THE DOMESTIC CRICKETER

MEMOIRS

by

Dick Redbourn

MIDAS BOOKS

Dedicated to:
St. James's C.C., Brighton,
The Alderman and Moo

J. Hindmarsh

'The front cover captures the author playing a perfect forward grope'

First published 1977 by
MIDAS BOOKS
12 Dene Way, Speldhurst,
Tunbridge Wells, Kent TN3 0NX

© Dick Redbourn 1977

ISBN 0 85936 093 8

Printed in Great Britain by
Chapel River Press, Andover, Hampshire.

Contents

Acknowledgments

So many club cricketers, wives and friends have offered their enthusiastic support for this venture that the consequences of failure became positively frightening (*see Boyd-Pain, Ch. 3*).

My thanks to all and especially:

My parents and family.

Dick Sankey of the George and Dragon, Speldhurst, for the introduction to Midas Books.

Ian Morley-Clarke of Midas Books, for sheer courage.

Norman Harris and Robin Marlar of the Sunday Times.

Gary Franses of the Brighton and Hove Gazette.

Noel Bennett, who kindly allowed me to ply him with ale while he reminisced.

Eric Hilson, Arthur Burridge et al, for valuable historic material.

Don Bates and Tony Greig, for enthusiastic and unselfish support.

Robin Forbes, formerly of Mayfield C.C.

Preston Nomads C.C. and in particular President Spen Cama, Bert Bridle, John Franks, David Laing and Roy Bowerman, for much assistance and use of their Ground at Fulking for photographs.

John Hindmarsh, for the superb cover shot and other photographs.

The County Ground Saturday Morning Club.

The Sussex Championship League, whose players and officials have offered great encouragement. Member clubs are: Arundel, Bolney, East Preston, Felpham, Goring, Hailsham, Horley, Hove Montefiore, Ifield, Littlehampton, Pagham. Portslade, Rottingdean, St. James's, Shoreham and Southwick.

Tribute

To the playing members of St. James's Cricket Club, Brighton, who:

> 'conceived in 1974 and subsequently sophisticated, the esotericism* termed *domesticity*.'

David Atkins, Bill Bailey, David Beaver, David Bell, Nick Betteridge, Ian Boyd-Pain, John Butt, Tony DaVall, Peter Davis, Andy Driver, Tony Flood, Paul Gaskell, Peter Gaskell, Chris Gibson, Roger Green, Charles Harrison, Ian Heath, Nick Holmes, Bruce Lowe, John Moore, Philip Parsons, Derek Pickering, James Puttington, Geoff Stern, David Stewart, Peter Sturges, Tony Sweetman, Huntley Taylor, Chris Terleski, Brian Voyle-Morgan, Ken Watkins, John Wensley, Ken Wensley, Richard White, Mark Whitlock, Peter Withers and Nick Wright.

O.E.D. pp. 894.

Line drawings of W. G. Grace by Harry Furniss (1854-1925)

Foreword

Club cricket cannot be ignored—it is fundamental to the structure of the game in this country. Here is an enjoyable romp through those long summer days depicting all the humour, devotion and even serious intent attached to the club game. But most of all the humour: the author bases his book upon the concept that there are two categories of Club cricketer—stars and domestics—which he defines in some detail. The word *domestic* emerges from the French *domestique* cyclists who 'pedal their hearts out day after day to set the pace and provide protection for the stars who sprint over the line at the finish and scoop up all the adulation, cash, publicity and spare crumpet'.

Some of the author's stories may sound stranger than fiction, ranging from the dedication that saw through to completion the Mayfield Tour—surely the ultimate in adversity—to the winter Sunday ritual carrying on nearly into November, all in aid of one man's quest for a thousand runs for the year.

The characters that emerge—from The Alderman, a fanatical cricket enthusiast, to the stylish incomprehensible B.P.; from Puttie, the gentleman cricketer, to the lovable rotund Christmas Day hero, Noel Bennett—are all, one suspects, lurking in some form in every club throughout the land.

This is a book for all, but particularly for those who have played or followed the game at any level. Without hitting the headlines, the author has clearly enjoyed immense fun and comradeship over the years, which must surely be a real incentive to any school-leaver wondering whether to take up or continue playing cricket.

Signed

A. W. Greig (Capt. Sussex and England)

Preface

As one publisher said while rejecting my manuscript: 'In any case, what do you want to write a book for—just an ego-trip?' Well possibly that's true, but while I have my ego-trip, I can at least express the hope, however pious, that readers enjoy my cricketing 'memoirs' despite the absence of any literary merit.

It is certain that my style of humour will not appeal to all but I beg the reader to accept that I have written entirely without malice, vindictiveness or contempt towards anyone. Indeed, I regard James Puttington (whose superb sense of comedy I have highlighted in Chapter 7) as one of my greatest friends, a feeling I am confident is not entirely one-sided.

By way of explanation—it may appear that I have suddenly 'gone fictional' in Chapter 5 which concerns an extraordinary cricket enthusiast whom I have called simply 'The Alderman'. Though selected, the stories detailed in this chapter are true, but because The Alderman died some years ago and I am unacquainted with his family, I feel it advisable not to name names in case my affectionate potted biography be misunderstood.

As most of the action revolves around my club—St James's C.C., Brighton—I may give the impression that the playing standard, behaviour and organisation 'leave something to be desired'. To put the record straight: St James's have been, at various stages of their 78-year history, one of the strongest and most respected club sides in the county. This was especially true during the heyday of our President, A. K. 'Keith' Wilson, who was undoubtedly the finest Sussex club cricketer of his generation.

There are two people to whom I would like to offer my personal and special thanks:

David Benjamin who, as Captain of the Club when I first played, was extremely kind and generous to a shy awestruck teenager.

Derek Pickering, the current skipper whose brilliant reading of my 'Memo' in April, 1975, started the ball rolling and who has since been a constant source of encouragement, enthusiasm and practical help. (Good grief; if that doesn't push me a few places up the batting order, nothing will!!!)

Oh—and there's the wife. Thank you wife.

Dick Redbourn,
Crowborough, Sussex.
January, 1977

P.S.—Aside from the many errors, I have included one deliberate mistake which I invite students of Sussex club cricket to find. I am delighted to announce that a half-pint of ordinary bitter awaits the lucky first person to tell me.

By Courtesy: Sussex Life

Cricket at Stanmer Park, Brighton

Note first slip in determined and aggressive stance

1. *The Formative Years*

I thought that a suitably grandiose title for the first chapter would help to cover up the fact that this is my first venture into print. Indeed, the most difficult thing I've written up to now is that monthly letter to the bank manager explaining how it happened, and assuring him that it won't happen again. May I apologise therefore in advance for the style, or rather lack of style, of these memoirs and hope that the reader will find the patience to wade through the literary garbage and enjoy the various incidents and stories related from my experience in local club cricket.

Dare I suggest that cricket literature is top heavy with ghosted autobiographies of the County and Test stars and this is an attempt to redress the balance by coming from what is politely termed 'the lower echelons' of the game. In addition, my motives in putting pen to paper are to highlight the frustrations facing that happy band of less talented but loyal team men whom I define later as *the domestics*. As the editor of Wisden has not shown any great interest in my career I must first sketch in a few details to enable you to grasp fully what a complete nonentity I am in the cricketing world. Before doing so, however, I must not be too modest to omit to mention the three facts which do lift me a little above the common horde.

Firstly, I am a direct and reasonably legitimate descendant of Jem Broadbridge who starred for Sussex against England in the famous series of matches in 1827. Secondly, I share the same birthday as Sir Donald Bradman which, as my so-called colleagues are quick to point out, is exactly as far as the resemblance goes. Thirdly, at the time of writing, my career batting average on the County Ground at Hove is 85. This would appear to bear comparison with the English record held by a certain Ranjitsinhji who averaged 56 playing for Sussex around the turn of the century. I don't feel it necessary to mention that I have played only one innings on this hallowed turf.

I arrived in the world at Brighton in Sussex when the Dorniers and Heinkels were droning overhead and I suppose it mirrors the circumstances prevailing nowadays when the skipper decides to send me to the wicket. My father, always keen on the game, did his bit in the back garden and I first played in matches in my last two years at primary school. Since then I have performed more or less every summer weekend in school or club cricket, generally in the Sussex area. I managed to negotiate the 11-plus and went to Varndean Grammar School in Brighton where I was lucky to come under the influence of Noel Jones and Jimmy Foster, both first rate club cricketers, who played a number of games for Sussex 2nd XI. Noel used to bowl off and leg cutters which he pushed through with considerable spin, while Jimmy bowled slower, more flighty off-breaks. I played in the various school teams through to the sixth form and cannot remember any details, not that they would be of the slightest interest to anyone. But I do recall, with affection, Physical Education lessons given by Noel Jones.

We had two forty-minute periods a week of P.E. and the class of thirty would get changed and assemble in the gym, ready for action. In the winter months, Noel would have us hanging on beams and jumping up and down on benches fairly energetically, but in the summer term it was a different story. He would stroll into the gym after we had changed, toss a tennis ball from hand to hand and say, 'Right then lads, what do you want to do today?' As all sorts of naughty thoughts crossed our minds, he would add, 'How about some cricket practice?' Without further ado, he would detail someone to fetch 'the bat', which was an old blade shaved down on both sides to about two inches width, rather like a square-edged baseball bat.

The first nominated batsman would then take up a stance in front of a wicket, chalked on the wall, while everyone else spread themselves round in a circle about a foot apart. Noel would then operate off a three-yard run-up pushing the ball through quickly and turning it at least a yard. It should have been good practice for a budding batsman, but survival was usually limited to an over, or less. Because of the bounce, narrow bat and vicious spin, anyone able to connect with a forward push would invariably be caught by one of the dozens of close fielders. One's only hope therefore was to play a full blooded drive, and hope the ball would bounce off someone's shins. After a forty-minute session Noel, bowling unchanged, would I suppose have taken about 28 wickets for 10 runs off 15 overs.

Jimmy Foster taught chemistry and my main recollections of him, in the cricket sense, are of the school playing the Staff XI when he would operate with immeasurable guile from the bottom end. Chemistry was not my favourite subject and I have the examination results to prove it, but I do remember a lesson near the end of the summer term one year.

It was a hot day after the exams and being shut in a dark and smelly chemistry lab was pretty boring to everyone—including, I believe, Jimmy Foster. He paced slowly up and down one side of the lab, tapping a long ruler against one leg and the instruction, spread over a quarter of an hour, went roughly like this:

'Now then lads, base + acid = salt + water' (long pause).

'Bloggs, what does base + acid equal?'

'Salt + water, Sir.'

'Correct, well done Bloggs, excellent. First class. Salt+water' (very long pause).

'Right now lads, let me give you an example of this principle' (very long pause).

'Er . . . Ummm, what am I going to do, Smith?'

'Give us an example, Sir.'

'Ah yes that's right. Well done Smith, good lad, excellent' (pause).

'Ummm . . . , now let me see. $N_aOH + H_2SO$—four through the covers. Great shot. Well played, Sir! ! !'

As he got to the four in the formula he adopted a batting position and then sprang into an elegant cover drive, neatly bisecting the gap between the test tube rack and the fume cupboards. Having held his position with imaginary bat across shoulder for a few seconds, he then assumed the role of spectator clapping enthusiastically from the boundary. He soon came out of his trance, and apologised for his flight of fantasy and returned reluctantly to the matters in hand. As I remembered that formula without reference to text books, it proves that he got the message over, as well as illuminating a dreary afternoon.

I stayed on at school until the sixth form and went on to university (very much the done thing at that time) and also ventured into club cricket as the complete green-horn. Those early games seem light years away now, and I can remember nothing except that I was keen to score runs and able to rush about athletically in the field. Nevertheless, there were a couple of incidents which started to open my eyes to the big wide world of gamesmanship and the role of the domestic cricketer.

I vaguely remember playing with a number of mates for a local club in an evening match against a side of seasoned players. We were fielding first, and being young, fit and enthusiastic, we did all sorts of ridiculous things, such as diving to stop the ball, picking up and throwing in one movement, and chasing the ball all the way to the boundary. A chap of about fifty came into bat in the middle order after we had had some success and quickly sized up the situation. After two or three balls he called a mid-wicket conference, and thereafter the two batsmen proceeded to acquire runs at an alarming rate. They would push the ball into the covers or mid-wicket area, take two or three steps down the track before hesitating in apparent quandry calling, 'Yes, no, wait, come on, run one.' As the batsmen kept a sharp eye on the ball, we rushed in, fielded and hurled at the stumps like demented javelin throwers. When I came to my senses after the innings, I worked out that they had scored a third of their runs with overthrows!

Not having a regular club, schoolboys were obvious material for fill-ins by local clubs a bit short during the holiday period. On one occasion a team secretary asked three of us to play and his instructions were short and to the point:

'The game is at Ashford, Tuesday, 2.15 start. Make your own way there.'

Without a car it was quite a trek on public transport and, in fact, only two of us arrived at the ground in Kent, as the other chap had set off for Ashford in Middlesex and was not seen or heard of again for a day or two. Also, I fielded at fine leg both ends, was number nine in the batting order, didn't get a knock, and was then charged full match fee and tea money.

Those incidents heralded the start of a long and undistinguished club cricket career. I joined St. James's C.C., whose home ground is at Stanmer Park, Brighton, and have maintained a place in the side as one of the less outstanding performers, while doing the usual chores such as team secretary, fixtures secretary, and so on. Most of the skills and techniques of club cricket which I detail in this book have been gleaned while playing for this Club, established in 1898 and still going strong.

Looking back now, some fifteen years and several hundred matches later, I can only remember the vaguest details of results, runs scored or time and place, but burned in my memory are a host of trivial, ridiculous or unusual incidents which may conceivably be amusing to others.

In case any reader is frightened that I am about to embark on a long catalogue of my personal performances, I propose to mention just one and one only. As yet I have only once scored a ton and one would think therefore that I could replay every shot in my sleep. In fact, all I can remember was being dropped when I was forty odd, having skied the gentlest of lobs to cover, who tried to embrace it like a long-lost friend, then fell on to the point of his shoulder and writhed on the deck in agony, whilst we dashed up and down for a crafty two. Even the exact score I made is in doubt as Puttie (*see Chapter* 7), acting as scorer at the time, puffed heavily on his pipe while trying to keep up with my elegant stroke play and blew a red hot cinder on to the score book. This caused a minor conflagration, and destroyed some of the vital evidence. ('Bother me, I'm terribly sorry old boy.')

I was once told by a doctor carrying out some intelligence tests, that whilst I was reasonably well equipped generally, he was amazed to have proved beyond scientific doubt that I have absolutely no imagination at all. You must accept therefore that all the stories in this book are basically true, sometimes with a dash of spice added, although the chronology, places and performers are certainly well mixed up.

But firstly what is a *domestic*?

13

2. Domestics

May I suggest that cricketers at the top level rushing round the world from Test Match to Test Match never enjoy, and perhaps are never aware of, the subtleties of the game at club level. To illustrate my point may I offer the following situation. England versus Australia Fifth Test at the Oval, struggling at 48 for 4 and Dennis Lillee having taken three quick wickets, is waiting at the end of his run-up for the new batsman to face up. Imagine his reaction on starting to run in, seeing the batsman wearing dirty grey plimsolls, one pad and no gloves, standing about two feet outside leg stump!

In fact, of course, without looking Lillee knows that the incoming batsman will be blond, 6ft 7½in tall, stand upright at the crease, and that consequently he will have to bang in his first bouncer precisely 3½in shorter to reach his chin.

Part of the delights of club cricket is that often one never knows how good the opposition are, what the pitch and outfield are like and whether the umpire is bent or simply incompetent—or indeed, whether there will be an umpire at all. By studying these aspects of the game, unlimited scope for humour is available to compensate for dreary hours spent knee-deep in wet grass, watching the opposing batsmen stone-wall long-hops and full-tosses.

The first and most important assessment to be made when turning up for a match is the strength of the opposition, and to this end performers can be conveniently divided into *Stars* and *Domestics*. The term *Star* is common to many fields of activity and I would define its application to club cricket as a player who expects to play a major part in the proceedings and thereby influence the result. As a batsman he would have scored a number of fifties and perhaps a few tons in the past, and even if going through a bad patch knows that it's only a matter of time before runs will begin to flow again. As a bowler a Star expects to pitch 'there or thereabouts' from the word go, concede at most three or four runs an over and is blasé about taking fifty or a hundred wickets a season.

The other category of performer hereby termed the *Domestic* can be generally defined as a player who does not expect to score runs or take wickets and thus knows that his presence in the side will make no appreciable difference to the course of events. A Domestic is not a fill-in, but a regular club member experienced and philosophical enough to accept that his cricketing limitations will prevent him from grabbing the glory. He also knows that his presence is essential, or there would be no pitch prepared, no sightscreen or boundary markers and certainly no teas.

I am indebted to my team-mate and fellow sufferer Tony DaVall, who coined the term from the French *Domestiques* who take part in long distance cycle races like the Tour-de-France. *Les domestiques* are the average team cyclists, who pedal their heart out day after day to set the pace and provide protection for the stars who, when it really matters, sprint over the line at the finish and scoop up all the adulation, cash, publicity and, no doubt, spare crumpet.

I readily include myself in the vast army of anonymous Domestics, the term of course being relative to a particular team or level of cricket. But note that by definition, a Domestic is unambitious and therefore not interested in moving to a lower grade or weaker side in order to become the star performer.

The many subtleties of Star and Domestic status will, I trust, become more apparent as you struggle to read on, but I sketch below the arrival and preparation for a match of two typical club cricketers, Joe Bloggs and Gerry Larman. Needless to say, there are no prizes awarded for sorting out the Star and the Domestic.

Joe Bloggs arrives at the ground by bus, clutching his kit, which is spilling out of a small tatty hold-all. Knowing he will have to set up the sightscreen, etc., he rushes eagerly into the club house to change, and nodding politely to his colleagues, tips his kit from the hold-all. His boots immediately rivet the attention. Showing no sign of whitener, they possess three worn-down studs and are held together by a knotty lace dodging between the few available eyeholes. Joe's wife has not had time to iron his cricket shirt, so he dons a short-sleeved one, flecked with blue emulsion, and then puts on his cream sweater with roll necked collar. His flannels indicate a scarcity of fly buttons, but to compensate there are plenty of creases and grass burns.

His skipper announces that they are batting, Joe is relieved to find that he is down the order, and relaxes while the openers pad-up. When the moment eventually arrives for Joe's knock, he returns to the dressing room and slips a pink plastic box furtively down the front of his trousers. Searching the club kit he manages to find two pads complete with all buckles, although unfortunately they are not a pair. Sorting out two gloves looking fairly similar, he produces his bat, of dark brown hue, bound together by much tape and string. As he waits nervously for his call to action, he practices, somewhat self-consciously, some aggressive air shots. At the fall of the wicket he marches out bravely to the stumps asks for 'middle' and takes a quick look round the field before facing up to his first ball. From then on, with Joe's fate firmly in the lap of the Gods it's all grope, tonk, swipe, smear, lunge, smash, ya-hoo, hoik, edge, fend, heave and snick.

Gerry Larman is a different kettle of fish. He arrives at the ground a fraction late, pulling up sharply near the pavilion to draw attention to the attractive dolly bird in the passenger seat. His hair is fashionably long with greying sideburns and he sports a white neckerchief with his dark blue blazer. Greeting everyone cheerily, Gerry unloads his kit, consisting of a huge brown suit-case, several bats and a clothes hanger laden with freshly laundered shirts and flannels.

Showing no inclination to change, he wanders around chatting amicably until the skipper tells him to pad-up and to go in at number three. Spreading the contents of his suitcase around the changing room, he selects a clean shirt and an older pair of flannels, heavily creased below the knee, and puts them on without interruption to his chat. Next he finds his box, a massive metal and faded leather object, dented and festooned with straps, and puts it on, standing ostentatiously in the centre of the room. With trousers around ankles, he displays both his virility and the results of his valour in action. Having donned pads—his own of course—he selects one of several bats, sand-papered, clean and white with rubber grip fixed in position by sticky tape. He completes the exercise by carefully positioning a cap on top of his cultured locks, leaving several others wrapped in polythene bags, unwanted in his suitcase.

Wandering outside he spurns the offer of a knock-up, instead cadges a fag, before settling comfortably into a deck-chair. Waking up a dozing colleague, Gerry engages him in an enthusias-

16

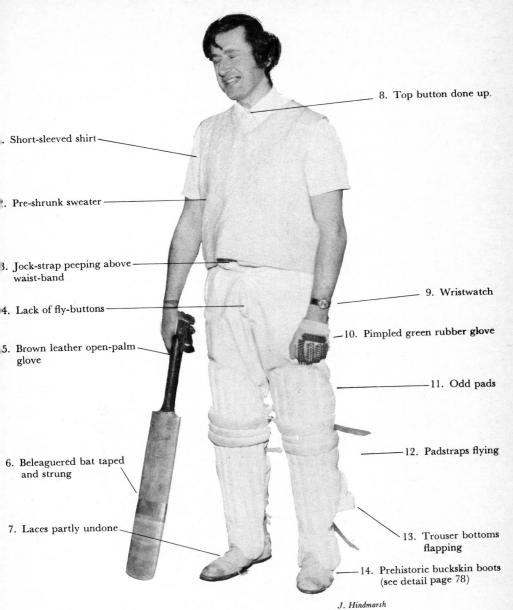

1. Short-sleeved shirt

2. Pre-shrunk sweater

3. Jock-strap peeping above waist-band

4. Lack of fly-buttons

5. Brown leather open-palm glove

6. Beleaguered bat taped and strung

7. Laces partly undone

8. Top button done up.

9. Wristwatch

10. Pimpled green rubber glove

11. Odd pads

12. Padstraps flying

13. Trouser bottoms flapping

14. Prehistoric buckskin boots (see detail page 78)

J. Hindmarsh

Joe Bloggs—The ultimate 'Domestic'
(Effortlessly modelled by Tony DaVall)
Apart from the air of false nonchalance note above

17

tic, if one-sided, conversation about the remarkable improvement in his putting. At the fall of the wicket, Gerry saunters onto the field still puffing his fag and makes for square-leg where he carefully grinds it out, while passing the time of day with the umpire. Continuing to the wicket he pops some chewing gum into his mouth before fixing his gloves into position. He takes a quick glance at the crease, then wanders down the track, gently prodding down some imaginary divots. He then goes back to the crease calling a casual, 'Two please umpire', over his shoulder. After making his mark, he draws a line from the stumps with the toe stud of his boot and next takes a cool measured look around the field. From this point, with Gerry firmly in control of events, it's all poetry as he proceeds to push, clip, hammer, stroke, force, guide, caress, punch, steer, ease, persuade, flick or coerce the ball around the park.

Joe Bloggs and Gerry Larman are, in fact, an amalgam of various real life characters, and most players fall somewhere between the two extremes. As you can see, *Star* status involves dress, style and above all, confidence, qualities lacking in the mature *Domestic* who has learned to recognise and accept the facts of life.

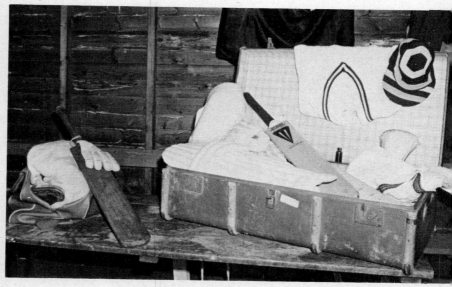

J. Hindmarsh

Which is Gerry's and which is Joe's?

Like many other clubs, St. James's have brought in a rule that any player who scores a fifty or takes five wickets must buy a jug in the bar afterwards. This rule is strictly enforced by the Domestics who seize on this opportunity to redress the balance. One or two players I know have developed a tendency to get involved in stupid run-outs when in the forties and the Star bowlers are now adept at sharing out the wickets, three or four apiece.

In spite of the internal tensions this rule causes and the ruinous financial strain on our Star all-rounder, on one point the club is completely united: the ultimate in Star status would be to arrive at the ground with your own pewter jug strapped to your cricket bag—initialled and heavily dented, of course!!

3. Basic Psychology

To state the obvious: psychology and gamesmanship are ever present in club cricket, and are particularly useful to the domestic player in covering up otherwise glaring deficiencies. There are countless ploys that can be used, from the juvenile trick of warning the incoming batsman of the devastating bowling that awaits him, to much more subtle and interesting territory.

Guesting, for example, is quite common in club cricket and has the clear advantage over playing for a regular team in that one avoids paying a match fee. But apart from that, a few timely and judiciously placed comments can enable the guest to select his place in the batting order or effectively put himself on to bowl. When asked by the skipper the inevitable, 'What do you do?' a possible reply is: 'I usually open the batting. As a matter of fact, I only need a dozen or so for my thousand this year.'

In similar vein, the guest bowler can put himself on with the casual: 'I bowl quickish. I'm just getting over some hamstring trouble actually, so a run out would be useful!!!'

Of course, these sort of comments have the nasty habit of rebounding disastrously, and apologies to the skipper can be tricky if you open the batting and grope forward to be castled first ball. To the mature domestic cricketer, there is only one

'Put 'em in Noel, put 'em in'

Noel Bennett (left) in action with coin at Gosport

answer to this question which avoids any possible embarrassment and that is simply: 'I don't bowl.'

Turning now to the specific episodes on the field of play, I intend to refer almost exclusively to two players and colleagues whom I consider were master exponents of the art of gamesmanship—Peter Beecheno and Ian Boyd-Pain. Both were expert at exploiting a situation when on top, and equally adept at face-saving exercises when on the receiving end. I intend to detail their handling and response to circumstances familiar to every cricketer, but before doing so it is necessary for me to sketch the characters involved.

At our first meeting Peter Beecheno immediately impressed me with his knowledge and experience of the game. Travelling by car to Gosport in Hampshire to play an all day match for Noel Bennetts' XI, Beech warned everyone that their opening batsmen were on the Hampshire Ground Staff and would have to be removed 'a bit sharpish'. When Noel Bennett went out to toss up with the Gosport skipper Beech went along as adviser, and while the captains exchanged pleasantries Beech stood deep in thought in the middle of the track. He then drew two fingers along the turf and stood pondering the result for several seconds. When Noel announced that he had won the toss, Beech called confidently: 'Put 'em in Noel, put 'em in'. 110 for 0 at lunch, the first wicket fell at 215, with one opener out for 108 and Gosport declared at 256 for 2 after the other opener had completed a not-out century. Since then, Beech has never been prepared to discuss the incident.

About ten years my senior, I've only seen him in operation towards the end of his outstanding club cricket career, but I know he started playing as a teenager soon after the war, mainly as a fast bowler. As the years rolled on, he became a more than competent batsman and steadied down to bowl medium to medium fast, and had the circumstances been right, he could probably have played for the county side in his hey-day. Indeed, looking back, one of Beech's fondest memories is of a benefit match arranged between a local team and the full Sussex County side at Hove. With Sussex batting first, their skipper, the late James Langridge, went into the visitors' dressing room and politely invited them to try their hardest, as the crowds were getting tired of beer matches and wanted to see a real contest. Beech, needing no further prompting, knew all about the famous

21

sea breezes wafting up from the south end and grabbed the new ball with relish. After Sussex had struggled to 50 for 6, a cryptic message was passed to the visiting captain via the incoming batsman to the effect that: 'the crowds are paying to watch Sussex bat, not Beecheno bowl. Take him off!!'

Beech was a cricket fanatic between 1950 and 1965 and usually played three or four games a week, scoring up to two thousand runs, and taking around 150 wickets a season. About fourteen stone and average height, he had distinctive large flat feet, and he expressed amusement by a deep throated chortle, which threatened to choke him if the situation developed. When put on to bowl, he adopted an air of businesslike authority in that he made it clear to the opposition that once the ball was in his hand, he was going to be in charge of affairs. Ripping off his sweater, he would enthusiastically pace out his run-up and then dictate his field placings with much shouting and gesticulating, all of which combined to put the batsmen on the defensive. This authority, which had grown from his undoubted ability and the results he had achieved over the years, was impressive to behold but in addition he had all the mannerisms to enhance the drama. He would shuffle up to the wicket off eight or nine paces and bowl with an ordinary if slightly round arm action, but he really came to life after the ball had been delivered. If he had taken a wicket or the ball had just been stopped by the batsmen, he would end up poised on one leg, bowling arm towards the ground in classic delivery stance. Alternatively, if the batsman had played and missed with the ball narrowly shaving the stumps, he would throw up his arms in dismay and remain for several seconds, arms in air or hands on head, in a state of utter incredulity, whilst emitting a succession of phew's, cor's, and ah's. Naturally Beech had a full throated appeal, but he also possessed the super emphatic 'How was that *then*' reserved for a second attempt against a particular batsman and also the more sparingly used desperation appeal, rarely turned down, which went: 'How was that then—this time, umpire—surely, please'. If he hit the pads when well outside the line he would end his follow through hands on knees, sideways to the batsman, peering down the line between stumps to indicate how close he had come to making an appeal.

Beech, never short of words or a quip in any situation was no respector of gentle manners. His shout 'Well left' must have been heard in every ground in Sussex and was his favourite riposte when the batsman had groped forward and missed one of his better deliveries. He used this cry to great effect and I readily recall a match at Chichester one year when the opposition contained a number of smart young chaps on vacation from college. The track was a bit fiery and Beech, revelling in the conditions, had ripped through the early batting when a very couth young gentleman came to the wicket. An electric atmosphere built up between batsman and bowler as events unfolded as follows:

To the first ball, the young gentleman played an immaculate forward defensive shot but failed to make contact as the ball pitched and whipped away late. Beech, with a broad grin called out the usual 'Well left', which surprised the young gentleman who clearly considered it 'bad form', but at the same time stiffened his resolve to get on top.

The second ball was an action replay except that it passed closer to the stumps on its way through to the 'keeper and Beech's comment this time was 'Well left again'. This caused the colour to rise in the young gentleman's face and he visibly gritted his teeth in determination for the next ball.

To the third ball the young gentleman groped even further forward as it pitched, cut back and whistled over the top of the off-stump and Beech, exasperated and virtually lost for words, could only repeat his 'Well left again', before shuffling back for his fourth delivery.

Yet again the action repeated itself but this time, having completed his arms in the air routine, Beech stood hands on hips, chuckling heartily before applying the physchological 'coup de grace':

'Tell you what old sport, you hold the bat still and I'll try and hit it!!'

I once had the dubious pleasure of batting against Beech and being 'psyched' out in a simple and charming way. Having just arrived at the crease, Beech came on and for two or three overs we sparred around as he tied me down with his customary accuracy. Suddenly he shouted out as the ball left his hand, 'Oh, sorry Dick, it's slipped'. This of course put the ball quite literally in my court as he'd announced to all and sundry that he had accidentally bowled a bad one, and therefore if I was any sort of batsman I would deal with it accordingly. Reacting like a startled elephant, I just managed to despatch a high full toss to the boundary and we continued in stalemate a while longer until he called out again:

'Whoops—sorry again Dick.' Of course it had not slipped and I departed bowled, having tried to hit a slow yorker out of the ground.

Another situation, especially familiar to domestic batsmen which Beech could handle with masterly aplomb, was that of being bowled first ball. A textbook example was a match against the Old Grammarians at Stanmer Park in 1965, when St. James's batting first had slumped to 28 for 4 with Beech due to go to the crease when, as he would put it: 'It's all gone dark'.

He bustled purposefully out to the wicket, bat tucked under arm as he pulled on gloves, exuding enthusiasm to come to grips with the enemy. Taking guard quickly without frills or fuss he took a measured look around the field, carefully noting the position of each player before facing up to the first ball. He pushed forward in pure coaching manual: elbow up, bat and pad together, front foot well forward and head down, but inexplicably the ball went straight through to shatter the stumps. Undeterred by the sound of falling woodwork, he retained his defensive position for at least five seconds with the clear purpose of demonstrating to shocked spectators that irrespective of the result, he had played the right shot and played it well. The fact that he had not made contact was a mere detail challenging the basis of Newtonian physics. Reluctantly, he abandoned the pose and set off for the pavilion shaking his head slowly from side to side in disbelief, but called out as he passed the bowler, 'Well bowled old sport. I bet you wish you could bowl that one again'. This apparently congratulatory remark was, of course, a subtle insult as it implied a fluke delivery.

Having sorted out the bowler, his next task was to allay the wrath of his skipper and to do this, he adopted a philosophically cheerful expression and before any comment could be made, he got in first with, 'Sorry skipper. I was waiting on the Northern Line but it came down Bakerloo!' (collapse of indignant skipper!)

Ian Boyd-Pain would be the last to admit that he was not in the super-star class of Beech as a cricketer, but what he lacked in that direction he made up for with style, panache and, to put it crudely, bullshit. If he ever appeared at the wicket in partnership with Colin Cowdrey, he would make the latter look positively domestic by comparison. Unfortunately certain other qualities required to make him the greatest batsman in the world, such as concentration and application, are not always present, but whatever B.P. does, it looks good.

B.P. is about my age with fashionably long hair and zapata moustache and, as a snappy dresser, has recently added a floppy white hat to his cricket gear, which along with his flared trousers tend to inhibit rapid movement in the field. Basically an all-rounder, he bowls off two paces with vicious finger spin announced by much wrist cocking, finger snapping and ball flicking, and given assistance from the track he has turned in some spectacular figures. More often he has taken wickets by driving the batsman to distraction with his antics, such as a delivery in our match at Storrington last year.

It was the third ball of the over and taking his short run up, B.P. turned too quickly for the batsman who was not quite ready to resume combat. B.P. stopped in his tracks, turned and went back to his mark, and then walked in very slowly as the batsman crouched in his stance, not certain whether B.P. was going to bowl or not. In fact B.P. was walking up to the crease to rub his hands in the dust around the bowlers footmarks to remove moisture. Having made a meal of this he walked back to his mark, turned and was about to run in when he hesitated, looked at square leg some 75 yards away on the boundary and instructed him to move one yard to his left. By now the batsman was showing clear signs of irritation but faced up again as B.P. started his run up. Having taken a couple of strides, this time he lost his rhythm and ran through the crease without delivering the ball. Offering a casual 'Sorry batsman', as he sauntered back to his mark, he finally bowled the ball to an opponent by then too frustrated to care, who executed a violent heave, only to hole-out at long-on.

By the very nature and definition of the term, the domestic cricketer spends in excess of ninety per cent of his active part in a match in the field and there are a number of useful ploys worth remembering on this subject. For example, in trying to make a catch the domestic player should assume that he will in fact drop it. An easy catch therefore should be disguised as half-chance, to gain full marks for effort from appreciative colleagues. In the close field the technique is to stand still as the ball comes towards one and then dive at the last moment trying to get both hands to it but always ending up full length on the ground. In the outfield it may be possible to feign non-sighting due to a dark background or 'sun in the eyes' but if another fielder is fairly near all that is required is an authoritative call of 'Yours!!'

The high altitude catch on the boundary is definitely one to be avoided and the recommended course of action is to run in soon after the ball is struck, pretending to misjudge the flight, and allow it to pass harmlessly overhead. If none of these options are open, then I suggest the fielder starts off sprinting towards the ball in determined style then engineers a trip with multiple somersaults to fall painfully to the turf. Skilfully done, this can earn praise from the skipper for valiant effort, coupled with sympathy for injuries incurred in the line of duty.

The act of fielding a ball struck along the ground can be deceptively simple on rough outfields and again much can be learned from the great Boyd-Pain in this direction. He excelled in being an extremely lissom mover, swooping one-handed to anything in his area. Unhappily, as most of his cricket was played on typical club outfields the inevitable result was that the ball popped up at the last moment to thwart a superb run-out attempt. As a co-fielder I've witnessed this situation many times and still wake up at night seething with fury at B.P.'s response to this predictable misfortune. Instead of turning to scamper after the ball to retrieve the misfield, he would stand hands on hips peering at the offending sod, before carefully stamping it down with the heel of his boot. Having conceded a further two runs carrying out this pointless exercise, he would saunter off half-heartedly in pursuit, if the ball had not already reached the boundary. The subtle point behind this charade was that B.P. was announcing that he was accustomed to playing his cricket on the smooth level surfaces associated with the top class game and that he was merely unable to adjust to more rustic surroundings.

Perhaps I can draw on my lengthy experience of fielding on outfields pitted with hoof marks or churned up with vehicle tracks, to advise on the best technique of stopping a ball struck along the ground into the deep.

Firstly, one must get into the general direction of the shot, not run forwards, but concentrate entirely on moving rapidly left or right to stay in line as the ball deviates from sod to sod. At the last possible second, having got behind the final estimated line, one drops onto both knees, keeping the body straight and

J. Hindmarsh

The author demonstrates the correct position for fielding a ball struck hard into the deep

head up. There are two techniques of stopping the ball which can be adopted at this point, depending on one's judgement of how predictable the last few moments will be, as ideally three hands are required.

One hand by necessity must be placed over the private parts and even the most devoted fanatics would not deny one the right to protect these assets. The other hand can then be used either to attempt to catch the ball or to protect the face until the ball has struck the body. As to which of these alternatives one adopts in a specific situation, involves many considerations including one's physical courage, team spirit and the cost of a new set of false teeth.

1. Old Blankonians cap

2. Upright starched collar

3. Sweater bottom tucked under

4. Handkerchief peeping from pocket

5. Sticky tape on handle grip

6. Sandpapered bat face

7. Lightweight boots for mobility

8. Hair fashionably long

9. Advertising insignia ta over

10. White neckerch

11. Sleeves roll below elbo

12. Sweatba

13. Thighp

14. Padstraps cut to leng

J. Hindmarsh

Gerry Larman—The ultimate 'Star'
(Effortlessly modelled by Boyd-Pain)
Apart from the air of supreme confidence note above

B.P.'s best performance demonstrating all the arts of one-upmanship was in a match against Petworth Park one year when, for once, the practical result matched the theoretical intention and he scored a magnificent and effortless 70.

Having settled in and scored 15, he was just beginning to see the ball well when he paused in mid-over and sauntered across to the square leg umpire to remove his sweater. When he reached 28, he dictated to the pavilion his requirement for a cap and when offered a choice of three, tried each one carefully before making a selection.

Soon after this, he demanded a fine adjustment to the sight-screen, but when he reached 40, he produced his master stroke. With the bowler putting down a good length delivery, B.P. jumped into the most perfect, effortless, cover drive which sent the ball humming to the boundary with the fielders stationary. While spectators were still gasping in admiration, he walked towards the pavilion waving his bat to indicate that it was not meeting his exacting requirements and therefore he wanted a change. After another protracted selection, with many testing air shots, he continued his innings to reach 50, thereupon, he took a fresh guard and moved on to his final ploy. At the end of an over, he walked back towards the pavilion and called out, 'I'm rather parched; bring out a glass of water please.'

B.P. was eventually bowled playing an airy cover drive which indicated quite clearly that he was becoming a trifle bored with it all, and someone else could now have a go. Listening to the rapturous applause as he reached the pavilion, I'm still not certain whether it was for the quantity of runs scored or the sheer style and arrogance of his performance.

For real super-confidence and one-upmanship, I must refer to an innings, played by a certain Andy Meads, a super-star performer, who carried at least half-a-dozen bats with him and had the complete professional approach. Before he went out to bat, he placed pieces of plastic foam between his toes on the right foot to prevent them rubbing together (his 'toe dividers') and at one stage of his career was advised by his doctor to wear special surgical paper under-pants to prevent jock-sore. To destroy any germs, these were ceremonially cremated after each match.

It is a fact that when batting once, he was into the eighties, when he held up the game while he called for a new left glove as the one he was wearing had 'sweated up'. But when he was 108 not out, with his side requiring just twenty runs to win in the last ten minutes, he held up the game and called for a brand new bat to be fetched from the boot of his car. I understand he felt he was then seeing the ball well enough to risk playing it in!!

4. Stag Dinner

An indispensable part of club cricket ritual is the annual stag dinner. It's all a matter of taste but the style of the cricket club dinner is quite distinct from the rugger club equivalent, in that the latter operates on a more elementary physical plane. A couple of jars of ale can be enough to set off trench warfare between rival factions with bread rolls and brussel sprouts being turned into missiles, and little or no attention paid to the efforts of the poor unfortunate souls press-ganged into speaking. At least at the cricket club dinner violence is for the most part of the verbal variety unless the speaker drones on too long when more desperate measures are clearly in order.

In a world where half the population is under-nourished, food throwing is clearly obscene. I have no pride looking back over my college days when I picked up many of the finer points of the art, and I seemed to spend much of the time rinsing gravy from my hair. Several remarkable events spring to mind. For example, every year the Junior Common Room presented a play in the Dining Hall when the Master and Senior Common Room were invited to attend. The play had half-a-dozen or so 'actors' who, after a couple of chaotic rehearsals, put on a terrible send-up of a scene from 'As you like it' or other such theatrical classic. There was only one showing of this spectacle and the audience from the J.C.R. arrived weighed down with bad tomatoes, rotten fruit and other offensive missiles diligently collected over the previous few days.

At the appointed hour, Senior Common Room staff would troop in fully gowned with mortar boards and take up their allotted places in the front row. The President of the J.C.R. would then thank the S.C.R. for their gracious attendance, announce the title of the play and retreat hurriedly as the curtain was pulled back. Before a word could be uttered from the performers, a barrage would commence and the actors, anticipating this, always carried a shield or dustbin lid for self-defence. For a few minutes the S.C.R. would sit through this mayhem until at a given signal from the Master they would stalk out in disgust covered in flour and vegetable matter. The next year precisely the same thing would happen, with the invitation to the S.C.R. coupled with profuse apologies about last year's debacle and assurances that such behaviour would not be repeated.

Another outlandish throwing event never to be forgotten was the Quinquereme which took place on the river each Annual College Day. Basically two teams of six each set out in a small rowing boat from opposite sides of the river with the object of capsizing the enemy by fair means or foul. Taken very seriously, it was a great honour to be selected for the crews and I still have an embroidered tie with dated insignia as proof of my participation. Each crew prepared carefully for the event by manufacturing an arsenal of missiles from such appetising ingredients as sheep's intestines, soot, rotten offal, sawdust, horse manure, etc. Considerable research and effort went into producing the smelliest and foulest concoctions possible which were then poured in a semi-liquid state into paper bags and sealed up to form a missile about cricket ball size. Incredibly, I recall there being a heated debate on the night before the event as to whether or not we should store the missiles in a refrigerator to prevent the pong getting too high, but it was finally accepted that in the frozen state fatal injuries could be caused to our opponents which was not really fair play.

When the great moment arrived we dressed up in old tee-shirts, shorts and plimsolls and taped on bathing or skull caps to keep our hair free from contamination from the opposition's missiles which we knew would contain similar ingredients. As usual, I was selected in a domestic role as one of the two oarsmen and my performance and contribution was brief and less than glorious. Our 'tactics' were to row flat out towards the enemy in an attempt to ram their boat while the rest of the crew threw missiles from the standing position, rapid fire, as soon as we were in range. Unhappily the first object that reached our boat from the enemy struck me a glancing blow on the side of the head removing my skull cap and depositing it on the water several yards away. Spurred by this to more aggressive action, I stood up, grabbed a missile in each hand and swung my arm back ready to commence an assault on the enemy. Unfortunately at this point a sheep's heart covered in soot and sawdust hit me smack in the mouth and I tumbled backwards into the river. Although not shark infested the river was certainly dysentery infected, and icy cold water and a mouth full of muck effectively terminated my interest in the event.

If I may be allowed to digress even further from my theme (stag dinner ! ! !) I seem to have spent a good deal of my academic career in or around the river. Another wonderful memory I have is of a challenge boat race between the soccer and rugger clubs over a quarter of a mile course. The race was with coxed fours and the Boat Club were understandably reluctant to lend their expensive craft to novice ham-fisted oarsmen. They eventually agreed with the proviso that each boat was controlled by an experienced cox whom they would supply. The contest was properly organised with correct dress and we carried the craft from the boat house, set it in the water and started to paddle a couple of hundred yards to the starting line.

Our cox was the traditional capped and bespectacled 8 stone figure, weighed down with sweaters, and while he shouted all sorts of complex instructions which we ignored, we hacked merrily away at the river shipping water at an alarming rate. Having travelled about a hundred yards and positioned in the middle of the river, we all realised simultaneously that the level of water inside the boat was equal to the level of the water outside. The instinct for survival took over and by telepathy we all stood up at once, dived in and set off for the nearest bank, while the cox continued his instruction to a non-existent crew. I have a wonderful mental picture, of glancing back and seeing the cox, water chest high, with his boat beneath the surface still shouting instructions through gritted teeth till he finally submerged leaving just his cap to mark the spot. He eventually resurfaced still clutching the boat and I believe someone was considerate enough to hold out a pole to assist him back to the side.

Having received all this expensive education it was only right that I should put it to good use and the first opportunities came at the Rugger Club dinners. Rugby has of course been trying to promote an image of respectability by holding formal and sober

32

occasions with local dignitaries much in evidence. This has not always been successful and there are many people who can recall the occasion when the Mayor walked out from my club dinner due to the loutish behaviour of just one individual out of a hundred or so impeccably behaved members. Having been politely applauded to his seat, we sat down after grace and for a few minutes a gentle buzz of conversation did nothing to ruffle any feathers. Then unforgivably some-one lobbed a bread roll, dunked in red wine, from the back of the room in a high trajectory which landed smack in the Mayor's soup as he bent poised, spoon to lips. Absolutely no-one was amused as he stalked out, tomato pips still dripping from his chain of office, and relations between the Town Hall and the Rugby Club once again went back to square one.

I got involved in a dangerous cross-fire situation at the Rugger Club dinner one year when the tables were laid out in the form of a trident with three legs branching down from the top table. Seated in the middle of the centre leg with a number of vice-presidents and other mature characters, a throwing war broke out between two groups, one on each of the outer legs. Experience dictated that I should keep my head down, turn my collar up and grin and bear it as missiles whistled in both directions overhead. I survived relatively unscathed for twenty minutes or so until a bread roll dunked in mushroom soup collided in mid-air with a soggy brussel sprout travelling in the opposite direction, and debris rained down on me like shrapnel.

This personal mishap aside, a few minutes later the leader of one of the combative groups produced a tactical strategem worthy of the Desert Fox himself. He stood up waving a white serviette and called across to his opponents, 'Cease fire chaps, must go for a pee.' With a flourish he left the room, went to a bar in another part of the hotel and bought a pint. He then crawled back into the dining room on all fours, pint in hand unnoticed by anyone, and went round the top table to end up behind his chief adversary. He stood up and remained poised for a few seconds with the pint over his opponent's unsuspecting head while he and the rest of us savoured the moment before pouring slowly.

My experience of Cricket Club dinners is of a different style with verbal rather than physical combat involved. I have been going to the St. James's dinner for some fifteen years and about eighty people sit down to dinner with the exuberant younger generation of players mixed up with former stars, relations and vice-presidents to give the occasion a sense of continuity. Our usual format is to allow four speakers about ten minutes each after the meal with the toastmaster throwing in various joke toasts to keep things moving. The atmosphere after dinner is unique; the air thick with cigar smoke and belches, and speakers must be ready for repartee from any quarter.

Naturally I can't remember very much of my first dinners, except admiration for the seemingly endless repertoire of jokes, although one speech sticks in mind. The speaker got up, said, 'Mr. President, Gentlemen', and embarked on the longest shaggy dog story I've ever heard involving a chap arriving at the customs and declaring two large suitcases which turned out to contain nothing but used French letters. After twenty minutes he finished and sat down, with his audience limp with laughter.

Of course the disadvantages of the type of speech involving blue jokes and four-letter words is that it often takes place while the waitresses are fussing around clearing up crockery or serving drinks and I've always felt uncomfortable when a motherly middle-aged waitress receives the punch line, a string of four-letter words, bellowed into her left ear. The trend nowadays is to use wit, sarcasm and double meaning and after all the whole point of a cricket club dinner is to talk about and around cricket, as events of the last season are of interest to vice-presidents and others.

Nevertheless, the subtle speech with too many private jokes can cause problems with the older generation perhaps a little hard of hearing and not so used to the late night session. To illustrate my point, I recall a speech a few years back by one of the players which was highly amusing to the younger set but the speaker was talking too quickly and quietly for some of the old guard who nodded off or muttered 'Speak up', in irritation. Suddenly one elderly vice-president got to his feet rather noisily and without any hint of recognition or apology shuffled across in front of the speaker towards the door, presumably for a visit to the 'gents'. Alternatively it could have been interpreted that he was staging a walk-out. One or two people chuckled at this unintentional insult and the speaker was clearly taken aback. But in a few seconds he recovered his poise and called after the old boy, 'Well surely it isn't that bad?' Again this comment went unheard

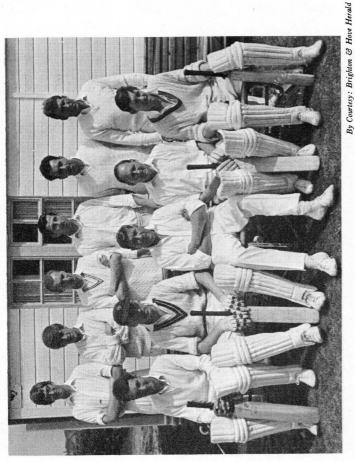

By Courtesy: Brighton & Hove Herald

St. James's C.C., 1968

Back row: C. Harrison, A. Shillaker, I. Boyd-Pain, I. Heath, R. Redbourn, P. Harbidge. *Middle row*: G. Stern, D. Atkins, P. Beecheno (Capt), J. Moore, D. Pickering. *Front row* (*standing*) : P. Beecheno's feet

35

and unheeded but with all eyes and ears focused on his retreating back, he produced the most devastating and effective riposte. He broke wind powerfully.

There's always difficulty in obtaining speakers for these occasions and it requires courage, especially for the younger members of the club, to make a speech before our highly critical and sometimes restless audience. I've made two or three speeches, the first one in particular went down quite well but one doesn't normally volunteer for the task. After the 1974 season when we developed the idea of the Star and Domestic sections in the club, I thought it might be an amusing idea if I sent a fictitious memorandum to the toastmaster at our Stag Dinner in April, 1975, detailing the finer points of the two categories. Derek Pickering acting as Toastmaster decided to read the 'Memo' verbatim and the reception it received was the 'inspiration' for this book. (An amusing footnote to this episode was that the Toastmaster made by far the longest speech of the evening !!)

The 'Memo' is reproduced below:

ST. JAMES'S C.C.
INTERNAL MEMO

Date: April, '75.

To: D. J. Pickering (Skipper).
From: Dick Redbourn.
Re: 'Domestics'.

During a match last season some bad feeling developed when someone remarked 'Watkins' innings was pretty domestic'. In retrospect the critic would have been better advised to use the word 'pedestrian', and I am sure than no insult was intended, or any doubt cast on Watkins' clear star status.

As with the 'social contract' there are no hard and fast rules for 'star' or 'domestic' status but as Secretary of the Domestic Section I have laid down guidelines which may be of assistance to all parties.

STAR STATUS

Generally a cricketer is a Star if he expects to bat and score runs and/or bowl and take wickets. He is therefore in a position to influence the course of the match.

A STAR BATSMAN:

Always expects to bat in the first six.

Draws a line with his boot when taking guard.

Wears a box.

Owns his own bat.

Always gets a 'dodgy' decision if given l.b.w.

Never misses a straight ball, but plays down the wrong line.

Sulks if run out.

Weeps and rages if run out by a domestic batsman.

Never swings or tonks, but strokes and pushes the ball about.

May refuse to play on certain dicey tracks.

Calls for a glass of water when he reaches 50.

A STAR BOWLER:

Is always 'there or thereabouts'.

Paces out his run up.

Has studs in his boots and peels off his sweater.

Has frequent trouble with his foothold.

Always has a red mark on his flannels.

Knows what sawdust is for.

Breaks down if knocked about by a star batsman.

Limps off in agony with a twisted ankle if knocked about by a domestic batsman.

DOMESTIC STATUS

A domestic cricketer does not expect to influence the course of the game, therefore bats or bowls only when necessary and knows his place.

A DOMESTIC BATSMAN:

Often asks for 'middle from where 'e bowls'.

Always edges the ball.

Gropes forward at least once an over and 'Ya-Hoos' frequently.

Cannot run more than 2 to any shot.

Falls over when sweeping.

Runs down the middle of the wicket and often collides with the other batsman.

May take a quick 'drag' between overs.

A DOMESTIC BOWLER:

Generally pitches within a radius of 10 yards of the batsman.

Wears a short sleeved shirt.

Does warming-up exercises after bowling a wide.

Appeals ecstatically if the batsman misses the ball.
Expects to be taken off after each over.
Calls a 'Donkey Drop' his slower ball.

Consequent to the above a domestic spends most of his time in the field and in this department he:
Is not expected to catch the ball.
Proceeds after the ball at a gentle trot.
Lobs the ball back in a graceful arc.
Often gets hit in the 'privates' while backing up.
Collides with a star who *was* about to make a great catch.
Probably fields at fine leg both ends.
Chats amicably with the square leg umpire.

In addition to the above a domestic cricketer:
Has to be early for a match, in order to do the chores.
Never cleans his boots or may wear dirty plimsolls.
Only speaks to a star when spoken to.
Always buys drinks for the stars.
Has to take the 'missus' home early.
Thinks a box is a 2 feet cube of cardboard.
Never gets the spare crumpet.

I trust the above notes will clarify the position of the Domestic Section.

Signed
R. A. Redbourn,
Dom. Secretary

5. The Alderman

In the early sixties I bumped into the most remarkable cricketing character I have ever met and am ever likely to meet, whom I shall call simply and respectfully The Alderman. He was the driving force and *raison d'être* of a local Council XI which started playing matches on a regular basis in the late forties and continued until the mid-sixties when the fixture list was whittled down to a few games a year.

The whole point of these matches was to foster friendly relations with neighbouring councils and mix council and staff in an enjoyable and sociable atmosphere. This of course was a fine idea, but in addition it provided so many astonishing and farcical incidents, that anyone able to write the complete history of the XI would be creating the definitive work on domestic cricket.

Eric Hilson and Arthur Burridge were regular local club cricketers throughout the golden era of the Council XI and probably know more than anyone about the history, politics and general goings-on of these matches, and I am indebted to them for much information particularly with regard to the earlier games.

The Alderman was into his fifties when he first played cricket, having been a tennis player of county standard in his younger days, and for some reason he became completely intoxicated with the game. Although he was the first to admit that he had had no coaching nor had any real idea how to play, he was always satisfied with his own credentials on the basis that he 'had a good eye and was as strong as an ox'.

Naturally I was not involved in the earlier games, but I understand that the side was made up in the beginning with half-a-dozen or so enthusiastic councillors with the balance made up of corporation staff drafted to fill-in. Councillors dug deep into their own pockets to pay a substantial portion of the costs of these matches played against neighbouring local councils and the various corporation departments.

Magnificent and valuable trophies were held by the winners

of the annual contest and I understand one ornate gold and marble creation is now worth thousands of pounds. Custody of the trophy for a match was entrusted to the Mayor's chauffeur who produced it from the boot at the appropriate time. The cricket played in those first matches was really just a diversion from cocktails, refreshments and social chat, and perhaps three hours' play would take place between eleven o'clock in the morning until stumps were drawn at six-thirty. The general format was cocktails on arrival at the ground, perhaps an hour's play before a magnificent lunch, another hour or so before an equally sumptuous tea, and then a final short session till liquid refreshment was laid on by a team of industrious staff.

As cricket matches the games were at novice level, as most of the players were well past the bloom of youth and some were making their debut on the field of play. Fielders tended to remain static and anyone who managed to stop the ball by stamping his boot or plimsoll on it was greeted with an enthusiastic round of applause. One rotund councillor, I understand, became quite adept at this fielding method but because of his girth was unable to bend and pick up the ball, so he would detail his nearest colleague to do this chore for him. On one occasion a lobbed catch was held by a fielder who pulled out the neck of his shirt and allowed the ball to drop safely down the front. On a more sober note, an over-weight councillor suffered a mild heart attack after attempting a risky third run, underlining the dangers of over-indulgence. If playing, the Mayor of course was always the star performer and would usually proceed to the wicket, accompanied by decorous applause, while wearing his gold chain of office.

As the enthusiasm of the councillors waned in the sixties it was necessary to bring in more corporation staff to make up the XI and The Alderman would have no hesitation on the morning of the game in phoning up Eric Hilson and instructing him to obtain six players for the afternoon's match. At this point I moved onto the scene, or at least the edge of it, through my connection with NALGO XI and various colleagues on the club cricket circuit. The set-up around this time was fabulous for the connoisseur, with the side made up of perhaps three or four councillors, some star fill-ins, plus a few domestic camp followers. In addition, there was always the spice of party politics plus a dash of class warfare to keep things interesting.

Most of the home games were played at that time in Finmore Park, a typically English idyllic setting for a cricket match. Entering through lodge gates off the main road, the drive winds through grass-land and trees for half a mile or so before bearing to the left of the pitch. Finmore House is set at the end of the drive and looking across from the house one can see the Church and pond with a large elm tree overshadowing the corner of the pitch and beyond that, farmland usually populated by vociferous cows. As the matches were usually held on a Tuesday afternoon there were rarely any supporters or disturbances of any kind to interfere with the ritual.

Parks and Gardens staff were very much on their toes for these matches and when The Alderman arrived in his elderly Rover he would be directed to a reserved place in front of Finmore House and would give the lucky groundsman a generous tip for carrying his kit, contained in a battered brown suitcase, up to the changing room.

I remember The Alderman at our first meeting as a big man with a solid paunch, unruly white hair and moustache, who walked with a slow shambling sort of gait. He sometimes arrived for the game half-changed, always with shirt buttons undone, often wearing a floppy panama hat, and in bad weather he donned a faded blue blazer but disdained the use of a sweater. He would greet all and sundry by their surnames, after, of course, he had passed the time of day with his fellow councillors and their good ladies. Everyone always addressed him as 'Sir' although he took kindly to being called 'Colonel' which I imagine must have re-kindled memories of his earlier days.

After the introductions had been made we would all troop up to the changing room and the game would commence more or less when everyone was ready, with no attention being paid to an agreed starting time. Having changed, The Alderman would toss up, bat first if possible, and although he was no cricketing tactician, he was not above applying some devilish cunning, and bending the rules when necessary. In this respect he had an understanding with the umpire, that if the council batted first he would produce an oldish ball which would miraculously transform itself to a shining new one during the tea interval, ready for use by the Council XI bowlers.

Another useful arrangement was worked with the chief caterer. If the Council XI were batting and things were not going

41

too well, at a given signal he would trot onto the pitch and announce that tea was not quite ready and would the umpires mind carrying on till five o'clock. This, of course, is the ideal situation for a Captain, with an agreed tea interval, but variable if necessary without agreement from the opposing skipper. In spite of this The Alderman always made it pretty clear to the opposition that he didn't approve of them batting on after tea whatever the circumstances. On one occasion, after a late start, the opposition were about 90 for 4 at tea and the skipper advised The Alderman that he was batting on for a few overs. Affronted, The Alderman replied that he couldn't, and that in any case he'd had the best of the wicket!

Teas were a sight to behold, usually scheduled for 4.30 and around four o'clock a huge pantechnicon emblazoned with the name of the local caterer pulled up at the side lawn of Finmore House and a fleet of waitresses and other staff disgorged complete with collapsible tables, chairs, sunshades, hampers of sandwiches, tea-making equipment and all sorts of other paraphernalia. A small marquee would be set up and all preparations made in the most professional manner with the caterer anxious that everything was either fresh or boiling at the right time. A top table was arranged with silver teapot, flowers and sunshade and this was graced by The Alderman and selected councillors plus the opposing skipper and anyone else of note invited to join him. Towards the end of tea The Alderman would rise to his feet and call for silence before addressing a few words to the assembled cast, thanking the opposition and all and sundry for a very enjoyable and exciting match, and looking forward to more fun in the second half. Then the opposition skipper would say a few words in reply thanking The Alderman profusely for the magnificent spread and hoping almost desperately for an invitation next year. Some skippers were quite nervous at this ordeal, composing fussy speeches which tended to prolong the tea interval, but things generally got under way again around 5.30, especially if the Council XI were due to bat.

Stumps were drawn at 7.15 or 7.30, depending perhaps on The Alderman's evening engagements or the state of the game, and more staff would arrive to set up shop with portable bar and crates of ale. The Alderman was a strict teetotaller so that when changed he would stay for just one glass of orangeade with the opposing skipper before setting off for home. Similarly the other councillors usually left quite quickly and this sometimes led to certain selfish individuals taking advantage of the facilities offered. I know for a fact that I played in the last match where unlimited drinks were available when a dozen of us got down to some hard socialising and finished off some 126 bottles of assorted ales and stouts before the barman, protesting about the excessive overtime he was clocking up, shut up shop. Unhappily as a result of this little episode someone took a cool look at the expense accounts with the inevitable result.

As already mentioned, The Alderman was no cricketer and relied heavily on the advice of his staff as to the conduct of the game. Generally he kept wicket and he owned a large pair of red gloves which showed little signs of wear as the seasons rolled on. This was due to the fact that he never cupped his hands but caught, or attempted to catch, the ball by slapping the gloves together at the right time. Not knowing at what speed his chosen bowler would deliver, he took up position some 15 yards back from the stumps, not crouching down but just bending forward from the waist. If he saw that the bowler was very slow he would stand closer up or even advance stealthily on the stumps if the batsman ventured out of his ground for any reason, even if only to do some gardening.

He once asked Eric Hilson why wicket-keepers threw the ball to slip or gulley rather than directly back to the bowler and Eric duly explained the difficulty of throwing the ball with gloves on and how this task is more readily performed by others. The Alderman took this to heart and thereafter would scoop or deflect the ball at random towards the slips automatically after each delivery. Unfortunately he did not realise that an understanding was necessary with the fielder concerned and some painful blows were received by unsuspecting councillors quietly day-dreaming the afternoon away in the slips. On other occasions runs were scored when The Alderman lobbed the ball absent-mindedly to a non-existent slip or gulley.

As a batsman The Alderman really only had one shot which could be described charitably as a leg glide, or a sort of backward shovelling motion with the feet unaltered from the stance position. As he claimed, he did seem to have a good eye and certainly scored a 50 on one occasion, 45 of which were steered past a frustrated fine leg off a bowler unable to control his inswing. His stay at the crease though was usually quite brief even with the customary 'one for the off', and he contented himself drinking in the scene prone from a deck-chair.

As a captain, his appreciation of cricketing tactics was rudimentary, but possessed of a certain logic and refreshingly simple. On bowling changes for example, he would put a bowler on for two overs which was extended to four if he got a wicket. After this he was taken off, either if successful, 'to give someone else a chance', or, if unsuccessful, 'to let someone else have a go'!

His batting order was usually councillors first in order of seniority, and also, perhaps, political allegiance, followed by star fill-ins and then anyone else whose name he could remember. Anyone unfortunate enough to be outside these categories (i.e., me) was allocated a number by one of his staff.

There is a huge fund of stories and incidents that took place in Council XI fixtures and I sincerely regret not having played in more than a dozen or so games. An appetising episode occurred at the very start of my first match played in Finmore Park when we were in the field. I forget who the opposition were, but our side contained a number of star fill-ins, including Derek Pokey, who was detailed by The Alderman to field at cover. As usual he was keeping wicket about 15 yards behind the stumps and the opening batsman, a chubby middle-aged domestic, faced up to the first ball. Our bowler pushed through a fairly friendly one which was struck powerfully into the covers straight to Pokey, who in his day was one of the best cover points in the county. The batsman, chuffed at making contact, made the typically domestic error of assuming there was a comfortable run in it and set off at a gentle trot down the track. By the time the batsmen were level in mid-wicket, Pokey, moving with pantherine grace, swooped on the ball and whistled in his return inches over the stumps at the wicket-keeper's end. The Alderman had not moved from his initial position and followed the path of the ball on its way to the boundary in astonishment. As I recall, he then rather crossly instructed first slip to take returns to the stumps as he presumably considered this chore best delegated to others.

Another memorable match was between the Council XI and the Transport Department, also in mid-week in Finmore Park. I particularly recall the game because for some reason I focused my attention on one member of the opposition, who clearly matured from a complete innocent, cricket-wise, to something more cynical during the course of the afternoon. Events started

44

Derek Pickering demonstrates a perfect 'swoop' (F8 at 1/1000 sec.)

with a bang as the Transport Department, not surprisingly, arrived in a double-decker bus, which looked somewhat incongruous parked alongside The Alderman's Rover in front of Finmore House. From first observations of the opposition it was clear that there was little cricketing experience amongst them as they hurried to the changing room, eagerly clutching new pairs of plimsolls, roll-necked sweaters and other borrowed apparel.

My hero, Bloggs, was at the time about 35 years old, thick set, bespectacled, with black greasy hair, and brimming over with enthusiasm like a small boy on a school outing. The Transport Department batted first and Bloggs came out with a colleague to open the batting, fairly well kitted out and organised apart from a lack of gloves. Bloggs elected to take first strike and as The Alderman decided to open with a star fill-in bowler I expected his demise to be pretty rapid. The first ball came down to which Bloggs executed a horrendous cow but to my surprise connected perfectly, sending the ball soaring over mid-wicket. Delighted, he set off down the track, bat aloft, like a scalded cat, while his bemused partner remained static at the other end. Hurtling towards the crease Bloggs made his first elementary mistake by trying to turn round on a sixpence, wearing plimsolls on a slightly greasy surface. Inevitably after various somersaults and other acrobatic motions he ended up in a heap approximately three yards past the wicket. His non-striking, non-moving partner now looked even more perplexed, torn between going to the assistance of his stricken colleague or attempting to gain his ground at the other end. He therefore remained rooted to the spot.

Bloggs had no such hesitations, bounced quickly back to his feet and shot off down the track to try and reach safety. As he neared his target he noticed the ball moving rapidly through the air from the arm of the retrieving fielder and was obliged to take a full length dive, this time with controlled acrobatics in order to beat the throw. The incident was not entirely over as the scorers came onto the field arguing heatedly as the Transport scorer thought at least one run was scored or should be awarded, whereas the more experienced Council XI scorer knew otherwise. The Alderman, called upon to arbitrate, acted with the wisdom of Solomon and awarded one run.

Bloggs made a few runs before he was castled, but another incident occurred later in the Transport Department innings when The Alderman called upon Councillor Dennis Smith to bowl the customary two overs.

As one of three councillors present he was readily distinguishable by his smart pair of brown suede Chelsea boots. He took the ball with impressive authority and carefully paced out a fifteen yard run-up, before attempting, unsuccessfully, to make a mark with the thick crepe soles of his boots. Giving that up, he ran in quickly to the stumps for his first ball but slowed down appreciably in the last two or three strides coming almost to a halt. He then produced the ultimate in 'Donkey Drops' to which the batsman, on a par cricket-wise, made a gigantic scything 'ya-hoo' and the ball continued harmlessly past the stumps. This action repeated itself a few times but then, as if determined to commit suicide, the batsman lurched several paces down the track before swinging the bat so violently that he ended up flat on his back, head towards the stumps, while the ball travelled in slow motion along the length of his body. It trickled up the wicket and tapped the off-stump with just sufficient force to dislodge a bail. Although lovely to watch, there was nothing unique about this incident, but what really appealed to my sense of humour was

46

The Alderman's congratulatory remark: 'Well bowled Dennis; just the breakthrough we needed.'

My next observation of Bloggs was at the start of the Council XI innings when The Alderman decided to send in two star fill-ins to open the batting against the suspected might of the Transport attack. The bowler set an unusual field by spreading his men at regular intervals in a circle, radius 25yd from the stumps and when things got under way our star batsman pushed forward to the first few balls while he took a look at the bowling. Bloggs, however, interpreted this as a sign of weakness and crept steathily in from his initial position until he was pretty close at silly mid-on. By the fifth ball, the batsman had fixed his sights and whipped a half volley off his toes straight at Bloggs who reacted like lightning by throwing both arms up into the air, both legs out in front of him and sitting down bolt upright on the deck. The ball screamed across the top of his head, parting his hair and leaving it standing as it roared off to the boundary. Bloggs, white-faced, trembling and mentally shattered, stood up, turned and walked halfway back to the boundary and remained static in that position for the rest of the match. His whole demeanour changed and he was subdued, almost sullen, when drinks were served after the game and I have a feeling that he never ventured forth voluntarily onto the field of play again.

'One for the off' was one of the great traditions of the Council XI matches (*see the Domestic Glossary*) and the arrangement was fine so long as it was understood by all parties; unhappily not always the case. An incident which springs to mind took place in a match against the R.A.F. Association one year.

The Alderman had cajoled the Mayor of that year into performing—I suspect very much against his wishes—and it was quite obvious that it was his cricketing debut. Nevertheless he prepared thoroughly for his ordeal, obtaining flannels, boots, etc., and much detailed advice from his officials as to the basic actions he was expected to perform. We batted first, and of course The Alderman asked the Mayor to open the innings with another councillor.

The Mayor, a tall upright figure, made his way to the stumps to take first ball and, as advised by his staff, held the bat in front of the stumps, and asked for middle. He shuffled the bat about a bit as instructed by the umpire but the advice he had received unfortunately had not stated that he had to make a mark

47

on the wicket, so he immediately adopted a passable stance and peered hopefully down the track. The bowler, by now poised for action, looked a distinctly star performer, complete with red mark on flannels, shiny toe-cap and carefully paced out run-up. Sitting watching all this from a deck-chair, I had a decidedly uncomfortable feeling at this point that the bowler had not been briefed, a feeling which turned to alarm as he accelerated smoothly up to the wicket and pitched the ball full speed on a perfect length. It whistled past the Mayor's off-stump missing by the proverbial coat of paint and thudded into the keeper's gloves, standing fully twenty yards back from the wicket. The Mayor, meanwhile, had not moved a muscle and continued to stay in his chosen stance while the ball was returned to the bowler. The second ball was an action replay with the Mayor still completely static, and the atmosphere became tense as we moved towards the impending disaster. By now the star bowler sensed he was on a good thing and hurried back to deliver his third ball which hit the Mayor smack on the front pad. The bowler rendered a tremendous appeal instantly turned down by the Council XI umpire, who was of course fully aware of the delicate situation.

The Mayor, grimacing with pain but managing to maintain dignity, resumed his stance, while our star bowler gritted his teeth, determined that such a set-back would soon be overcome.

Moving like an express train, he raced in for his fourth ball, again pitched on a perfect length and as straight as a die, sending the stumps cartwheeling in all directions with the Mayor still motionless. The resourceful Council XI umpire again came to the rescue, and seconds after the wicket was shattered while the bowler leapt around in jubilation, he called out loudly, 'No ball', and signalled ostentatiously to the scorer.

Prompted by some agitated signals 'off stage', the opposing skipper began to get the drift of things and moved across to have a 'quiet word' with his star bowler. The 'quiet word', however, was not effective and something of an altercation ensued, while it was made pretty clear to the skipper that our star played his game to win, came from Yorkshire, asked no quarter and was not interested in beer matches. The skipper was obliged to retire hurt, and fifth ball duly followed which once again completely shattered the Mayor's stumps. I think at his point he decided to withdraw before all dignity was lost and we all applauded dutifully as the Mayor reached the boundary. The Alderman advanced boldly, 'Bad luck Mr. Mayor', a sentiment I found difficult to endorse, although feeling sorry for the poor chap.

Undoubtedly my favourite incident on the 'one for the off' theme took place at Finmore Park in a match against the NALGO XI. The central character in this affair was a certain Councillor Bovine, a staunch Labour man of shop floor variety whose few words were explicit and often expletive. Aged about 45, he was a big man with paunch and black hair and I can't really think why he turned out for The Alderman, unless, to take the cynical view, he was mainly interested in the day out and hospitality like the rest of us.

The Alderman, having won the toss, batted first and things got under way in the usual fashion with councillors at the start of the batting order. Two or three wickets fell and the situation arrived where The Alderman was at the wicket at the non-striker's end, when Councillor Bovine came into bat. The NALGO captain and bowler at the time was one of my oldest friends, Brian Canter, a useful seam bowler who could move the ball away quite nicely. As a member of the corporation staff, he had played many games with and against the Council XI and needed no reminding of the traditional 'one for the off' rule. Like every seam bowler, Brian fancied his chances as a leg spinner, so the situation was ideal for him to toss up one for the new batsman. Councillor Bovine, wearing one glove and one pad and the inevitable plimsolls took guard and sunk into a static position awaiting developments. Brian took a couple of paces to the stumps and tossed up a speculative legger which, had the pitch been several yards longer, might have been a useful delivery. In the event the ball sailed full toss over the councillor's bat and hit the off-stump about 6in below the bails while he remained motionless. Brian was mortified, and Councillor Bovine seemed uncertain as to what had happened and what he was supposed to do next. Finally, first slip crept up to the wicket and whispered apologetically, 'I'm sorry, Sir, I'm afraid you're out'. The councillor started off for the boundary and his amazement slowly turned to rage when he realised that all his arrangements for an afternoon's cricket had resulted in about five seconds of real 'activity', As he was halfway back to the boundary The Alderman, leaning on his bat at the non-striker's end and watching the whole scene with an air of dismay and resignation, called out sympathetically: 'Not a very friendly one for first

ball, was it Councillor?' More than ten years later I can still
hear his monosyllabic reply, spat out with venom, echoing
across the empty stillness of Finmore Park:

'* * * * ! ! 6 * ! 6 ! * ! 6 * ! !'

It was during the period that I was filling-in for the Council XI
that Eric Hilson was coming under increasing pressure to find
players, always a problem for matches held in mid-week. Forced
to scour round every nook and cranny for anyone looking
remotely like a cricketer, some of his selections were less than
successful and this became something of an in-joke amongst the
regular players.

Eric still has nightmares about a young Ceylonese chap, who
got onto the Council during one of the periodic Liberal revivals,
and indicated that he had played cricket and would like the odd
game. Eric, delighted, fitted him in at the earliest opportunity
while tipping The Alderman that he had come across a real find.
The new councillor arrived late for the match and eventually
appeared at the side of the pitch dressed in colourful garb.
Undaunted, The Alderman called him on and immediately put
him on to bowl. Suffice to say, his first over consisted of twelve
balls including six wides.

On another occasion a Senior Officer had moved down to the
area from the North and had shown no interest in the sport until
he phoned Eric one day and told him that he had played cricket
in the Lancashire League and would like the odd game for the
Council XI if he could be fitted in. This was manna from heaven,
and Eric slotted him in the side immediately, but again illusions
were shattered when, on the day of the match, the 'Lancashire
Leaguer' emerged from the dressing room wearing a pale blue
roll-neck sweater, slate grey flannels and plimsolls. But there
was more to it than that: his pair of plimsolls were made up of
one black one and one white one! !

Even the old saying 'The devil you know, rather than the
devil you don't know', brought problems to Eric, as on the
occasion he invited a star bowler well known in local club cricket
to play in a Council XI match. There was no sign of the star
when The Alderman took the field, but he rolled up twenty
minutes late, clearly under the influence after a heavy lunch-
time session and, surveying the scene from the side of the pitch,
bellowed out, 'I'm here, Guv'—I'll take the top end'.

The Alderman was a man of great physical courage and furthermore seemed almost impervious to pain. I've seen him take some fearful blows as a wicket-keeper, as clearly in his later years he could not react as quickly to varying pace and bounce. There was an incident when standing back to a quick bowler the ball shot along the ground, hit the toe-cap of his boot flying about 20ft vertically into the air. As he got up from his bending position the ball came down on the top of his head with a fair thump, and everyone rushed in expecting to see The Alderman fall pole-axed. As it was, he simply retrieved the ball and lobbed it back to the bowler without in any way acknowledging the blow.

Arthur Burridge tells of another occasion when he was batting with The Alderman in an away match at St. Swithin's Hospital. The Hospital had a fiery opening bowler pinging the ball down just short of a length on a pretty uneven track. To one ball The Alderman pushed forward, but it flew up and hit him smack in the mouth with the force of the blow shattering his dentures. Again everyone expected him to fall or, at least, issue a cry of pain, but as the pieces cascaded into the wicket his only concern was to retrieve all of them so that they could be stuck together again.

Another of The Alderman's idiosyncrasies was that he believed cricket could be played in all climatic conditions and matches were never called off because of bad weather. His remarkable physical constitution meant that he rarely paid any attention to wind or rain and I think he refused to recognise that one's enthusiasm for the game could be dampened by having to stand at third man ankle deep in mud during a thunderstorm. Sometimes, though, he would at least acknowledge the existence of the elements and phone up Eric Hilson on the morning of the match with the instruction, 'It looks a bit wet today, Hilson; tell the men to bring their gum-boots'.

For one match, after two days of continuous rain, The Alderman pulled up at Finmore House at two o'clock to be greeted by the groundsman, shaking his head glumly from side to side. He poked his head through the car window and said, 'Terribly sorry, Sir, the game's off. The pitch is completely waterlogged'.

The Alderman's cheery reply was, 'Oh that's quite all right, we'll manage'.

Then there was the lovely picture of The Alderman, in shirt

sleeves, slumped in his usual position in a deck chair by the side of the Finmore pitch when a torrential cloud burst sent the players racing off the field to take shelter. Utterly indifferent, The Alderman remained seated and called out contemptuously after the disappearing players. 'What are you all made of then, tissue paper?'

One of The Alderman's favourite fixtures was the annual match usually in August or September against the officers and crew of H.M.S. *Hero*. The naval frigate always paid an annual courtesy visit to the town and dropped anchor a couple of miles off-shore for the weekend with various festivities arranged. On one particular year the visit was rather later than usual and it had been cold and wet, real wintry conditions in fact, for several days. With mountainous seas and gale force winds the Captain of the frigate decided it was too rough to anchor off-shore and went back to home base to take shelter. Naturally, he hardly gave a second thought to the possibility of a cricket match but phoned up on Sunday morning as a matter of courtesy just to confirm that the game was off. The Alderman, surprised by the call, confirmed that the game was on and the Captain had to commandeer a coach hastily and rush up to the town in time for the start. Hence climatic conditions which had defied the might of the Royal Navy had made no impression on The Alderman's game of cricket.

I feel privileged to have played in perhaps the classic all-weather match in the history of the Council XI. It took place in September one year at the Sports Stadium against a team raised by the Rotary Club and as my father had been a Rotarian for many years, I was drafted in to the opposition on this occasion. The match was in addition to the usual fixture list and considerable care had gone into the arrangements by both sides to ensure a happy and festive event. The weather, however, had other ideas and I will attempt to describe what happened in the following paragraphs.

On the morning of the match the sky was overcast from first light and by ten o'clock rain was falling steadily and, in the absence of wind, seemed set for the day. With the ground already soft with continuous rain from the previous few days, any normal match would have been called off by general agreement at mid-day at the latest. Nevertheless, aware of The Alderman's enthusiasm, everyone turned up dutifully at two o'clock and most of

BEFORE

AFTER

K. Wensley

'Some joker moved the —— sightscreen!'

us went straight into the bar for a few halves before closing time.

The consensus of opinion at this stage was that The Alderman would make an inspection of the wicket in the rain and be forced to admit defeat and call the game off. At 2.30 he waded out to the track and came back to announce, to our barely concealed surprise and dismay, that he thought things were improving and we would therefore take an early tea at 4 o'clock with a view to starting at 4.30. With a sumptuous tea in mind, we managed to stifle our derision and settled down to kill time.

In his speech after tea The Alderman referred briefly to the adverse weather conditions, but declared his confidence that a match would be held and announced his intention to carry out another inspection of the wicket. Squelching back from the middle, he stated cheerily that it was easing a little, and so everyone became resigned to the fact that a game was going to be played and got changed without further protest. We struggled onto the field in gathering gloom, with the rain sheeting down, and a number of players wore plastic macs and carried umbrellas. In the centre, bowlers with trouser legs rolled up fought to take a couple of paces to the wicket while batsmen floundered around like marooned walruses.

In those days an old bus shelter was used as a pavilion and as we sat huddled together waiting to bat, I focused my attention on one middle-aged Rotarian, perhaps playing his first game for years, and to understate—'unfamiliar with batting in a quagmire'. He announced with some pride that he had been shopping that morning to purchase new flannels, socks and plimsolls and how much he was looking forward to his knock, although he admitted that batting conditions were not ideal. His wife sitting alongside seemed nervous at the prospect of damage to his new apparel, apart from being generally wet and miserable. When his time came to bat he squelched out to the stumps and swished around for an over or two before meeting his demise, the manner of which was of some interest. After many wild misses he at last connected with a ball outside the off-stump sending it into the covers and set off delighted down the track. The non-striker, disinterested, called out a firm 'no' and our hero, attempting to stop half-way down the wicket, lost both feet and sat down heavily in the mud. Meanwhile having picked up and dropped the ball several times, the fielder finally managed to return it to the bowler's end which caused more havoc as he also dropped the ball and floundered around to pick it up. With The Alderman poised for action over the stumps, fairly champing at the bit, the batsman eventually scrambled to his feet and set off as fast as he could to regain his ground. Again, his enthusiasm thwarted him and he lost his foothold to end up skidding face downwards along the track, slithering to a halt just short of the crease. At this misfortune he gave up and lay there helplessly watching The Alderman, having fumbled the throw from the bowler, finally pick up the ball and sweep off the bails in triumph. The batsman returned to the pavilion an unhappy man, as his wife stood up wordless, her face a beautiful portrayal of shock, dismay and disbelief.

I understand The Alderman died aged nearly 70 in the late sixties not much more than a month after his last game—the annual fixture against H.M.S. *Hero*. I don't suppose he ever realised how much enjoyment he had given to so many people over the years and for me memories of those matches remain one of the highlights of my sporting career. I cannot believe that there has ever been, or ever will be, a cricket enthusiast quite like him.

6. Odds and Sods

Umpiring is often something of a bone of contention in club cricket particularly with the advent of keenly fought league matches. In some ways it is possible to divide umpires into stars and domestics as far as knowledge of the laws are concerned, but to be fair, the vast majority are competent and honest men doing the least glamorous job in the game. Nevertheless, as an over-critical and tactless player my inclination is to seek out those who could be classified as 'bent' or incompetent, on the basis that they provide the greatest potential for amusement.

My first introduction to a bent umpire came at a tender age when I was playing in an evening match at Patcham Place. It was a keenly fought limited over game and all I can remember is that the opposition batted first and scored about 85, and in reply with three overs left we were 78 for 7 and thus in a strong position to win. The opposing umpire was at the bowler's wicket when a ball was driven hard to mid-off standing square to the stumps. The batsmen set off on a suicidal run as mid-off fielded the ball cleanly, and swung round, arm poised to hurl at the bowler's wicket. At this point the umpire, realising that his life was in jeopardy, turned his back and ran a few yards away from the stumps. He dropped to his haunches, tucked head between knees, and remained cowering in this position while all the action took place. Mid-off hurled wildly at the stumps, stopped by a full length dive by the bowler, who then scrambled about on all fours to retrieve the ball before eventually breaking the wicket.

By this time, our batsman had comfortably made his ground but in the excitement of it all a tremendous appeal was unleashed. The answer was swift and clear as the umpire swivelled round with balletic grace, in a twisting corkscrew movement, ending up on one leg with index finger high in the air. Being youngsters the decision was hotly disputed to put it mildly, but since then I've always accepted philosophically the dodgy decision, on the basis that on average the good and the bad balance out, over a season or two. In fact I can only recall losing my cool on one occasion since then, when I went to sweep a slow long-hop and got a very thick and audible edge onto my front pad. I was peeved at being given out l.b.w. by their umpire, but got really hot under the collar with his reply to my polite suggestion that I'd hit the ball.

'Oh yes I know you hit it, but your leg was plumb in front, so you deserved to be out.'

Eric Hilson, who I mentioned in connection with the Council XI matches, assures me that he played in a match when the opposition umpire went right through the card. All ten of his side were given out l.b.w. and not a single decision given when Eric's team were in the field!

Eric also describes an interesting incident when batting in a match, when the umpire at the bowler's wicket was an elderly chap with a 'gammy' leg. Eric pushed the ball and called for a quick single which the non-striker refused after running a few yards down the track. So both batsmen, the bowler and a fielder with the ball all hurtled towards the stumps, and in the ensuing scrum the old chap, unable to take quick evasive action, was hit in several directions at once. Flattened, he was also dazed and concussed for a minute or two and a drink of water was brought on with the situation anything but funny. To everyone's relief he was finally revived, but as he sat up he lifted his finger and called out: 'He's out you know'.

To sort out the incompetent umpires, it is usually best to study mannerisms and style, in the same way that one can often spot a domestic batsman arriving at the crease. Occasionally though, all is revealed in a flash, as in the match I recall a few years back when we'd just put on our slow bowler. He took three or four paces to the crease and his first delivery was immediately called 'no ball'. Astonished, our bowler pointed to his front foot at least six inches behind the batting crease and queried how it could possibly be a 'no ball'. The umpire answered loftily, 'I'm not interested in that foot, your back foot was well over'. We worked out later that it was exactly three years after the front foot law had been introduced.

I love the episode of Sam, who volunteered to perform for NALGO in a match against Preston Nomads at Fulking one day.

At the start of the match with NALGO in the field, events got under way smoothly with Sam stationed at square leg for the first over. At the end of the over Sam remained stationary and still did not move when gently reminded by a nearby fielder. Tension mounted rapidly however, when the bowler was ready to perform, and Sam still remained at square leg. The embarrassed NALGO skipper was obliged to call out, 'Sam, you're supposed to stand at the wicket'. His breezy reply was, 'Oh that's all right, I can see quite well from here'.

If the Nomads batsmen were not trembling in their boots, then they should have been, because more agony was to follow. Eventually cajoled to the wicket, Sam stood there for a few seconds before he noticed that the bowler was 'left arm round' running in behind the umpire to the crease. He immediately apologised to the batsman and moved away from the wicket, proposing to walk, or perhaps run in alongside the bowler so that the batsman's view would not be obscured. I imagine the Nomads' batsman must have been dying to know whether Sam knew about holding his finger up!

Serious problems arise if you run into an umpire, both bent and incompetent, and I am pleased to confirm that I have managed to survive the experience. He was one of the old family retainer type of umpires who had stood for years, weathering visibly from season to season. A short, tubby chap, probably in his seventies, and always wearing a large cap, I first noticed him because he stood motionless, solidified almost, throughout the match. He seemed to do little more than act as a robot clothes hanger as sweaters were added or removed from his hunched shoulders, and my suspicions were aroused when I noticed that, when giving guard, he never called for any adjustment of the bat, but just waited a couple of seconds before darting his finger up and down to indicate approval.

Batting first in this particular game, he gave a couple of l.b.w. decisions against us which were not accepted with the best of grace. When it was our turn in the field, the several appeals we made were met by the umpire with stony indifference and no comment at all. Towards the end of the game, a batsman went right back onto the stumps, and missed a dead straight ball which kept low, and by all normal reckoning was absolutely plumb. The bowler and close field went into agonised contortions, with the roar deafening and deep square leg out-shouting everyone; but yet again no movement or comment from the umpire. Eventually we calmed down and the game continued, although I

Bent or incompetent?

'. . . he seemed to act as a robot clothes-hanger . . .'

heard two colleagues seriously debating whether on death it was possible to remain standing up, if rigor mortis set in quickly.

In the bar after the game, I felt I must find out a little more about this remarkable character so, pint in hand, I cornered one of their players and the discussion went as follows:

'Your umpire's an interesting chap isn't he?'

'Yes.'

'He must have been standing for you for a few years?'

'Oh yes.'

'He doesn't seem to give much, does he?'

'No.'

'We had one appeal for l.b. which must have been close, but he didn't seem to react at all?'

'Well he wouldn't, would he?'

'Why's that?'

'Well he's stone deaf. His eyesight's fading now as well. It's sad really.'

'Err . . . well, how does he . . . err—give decisions? After all you got a couple when you were in the field.'

'Oh, that's quite simple, he looks at second slip. If second slip puts his arms in the air he raises the finger. If not, no joy.'

This, of course, was staggering, and I was struck dumb for several seconds, my mind racing back to the situation when we made our last desperate appeal.

'Hang about, we didn't have a second slip.'

'Well that's your problem isn't it! ! ! ! ! ! ! ?'

I stored up this information carefully for the next year, but the old chap had perhaps retired or passed on by then.

Close observation of the incoming batsman with his style and method of taking guard is another area where important clues can be gleaned as to star or domestic status. A star batsman makes his mark with some authority and frequently draws a line with the toe stud of his boot, whereas domestics tend to be too finicky about the exact position of the bat. Many's the time I've seen a domestic give the game away by taking guard meticulously and digging a cavernous trench, then stand up, look around the field and plonk the bat down in a completely different place for first ball.

I can also recall some amusement involving that old chestnut, 'middle from where 'e bowls' (*see the Domestic Glossary*). We were playing in a match at Stanmer Park with Peter Beecheno bowling from the Church end, when the incoming batsman, a callow youth, quickly announced his domesticity by calling confidently: 'Middle from where 'e bowls'.

The umpire, amused, but sensing a chance for one-upmanship replied loudly to take the stage: 'I beg your pardon, Sir'. To this came the obvious reply, 'middle from where 'e bowls'. Clearly not a chess player, this floored the umpire who dithered for a few seconds before he tamely took a pace to his left and gave guard from there. Naturally Beech was watching all this with great interest and started to chortle to himself while displaying a mischievous grin. When the youth had completed his guard taking ceremony and the customary look round the field, he took up his stance for first ball and at this point precisely, Beech called out with glee, 'Umpire, I've decided to go round'. Peeved, the umpire dutifully informed the batsman who, disappointingly said simply: 'O.K.' and stayed where he was; the point clearly being lost on him.

Another enjoyable episode on this theme was of a chap who arrived at the crease and asked for 'just outside leg stump'. Tension mounted and everyone listened intently to the umpire's measured, even suspicious, reply which went:

'Just how much outside leg stump?'

At this, my adrenalin was really starting to flow and all sorts of incredible possibilities sprang to mind. For example, would he ask for some fantastic measurement like two and five-eighths inches? Would the umpire be forced to call for a tape measure, set square, protractor, chalk, string and other equipment? Would the batsman and the umpire end up on their knees at the crease earnestly discussing the square on the hypotenuse?

Unhappily it was not to be. After a pause, the batsman just shrugged his shoulders and called out: 'Oh, it doesn't matter', and took up a stance where he stood. Someone tackled him later as to what he meant, and in fact he wanted middle and leg which in a sense is 'just outside leg'.

There was a lovely first ball incident in a match at Fulking one year when the game was only just playable after days of heavy rain. Nothing much was happening and the game looked destined for a tame draw with my team in the field in the second innings. A wicket fell and the next batsman trailed out to the crease at a snail's pace possibly under orders to waste time, dragging his bat along the ground. Having finally got to the stumps he called for his guard, then set about the wicket with his bat and dug a massive trench to World War I standard. Not content with that, he also drew a line from the stumps to the crease with the side of his boot, and followed this by two angled lines to finish up with a large arrow shaped mark.

Next, he wandered down the wicket and carried out some energetic gardening with the back of the bat, flattening any sign of a divot over a huge area which would have covered any normal delivery and most wides as well. Finally, and reluctantly, he wandered back to the crease, looked around the field and would no doubt have asked for a sight screen to be moved had that been possible.

At last he faced up to the first ball and, as you've already guessed, he groped forward, left a huge gate and was comprehensively castled.

Everyone saw the funny side of this episode and started to chuckle openly, except the wicket-keeper. Surveying the general carnage and desecration at his feet he was not amused, and called out after the batsman as he wended his way slowly back to the pavilion, 'Tell the next bloke to bring a shovel will you?'

Of course there is always the story of the real rabbit performer, plimsolls, no gloves, possibly making his cricketing debut, who arrived at the crease and dangled the bat in front of the wicket. Pointing vaguely downwards, the following quick-fire conversation took place with the umpire:

'Wassat?'

'Two.'

'Two what?'

'Two legs.'

'Ha, Ha. Very funny.'

'All right then, middle and leg.'

'Thank you very much.'

7. Puttie

When I set out to write this book I immediately decided to devote a separate chapter to one of my greatest friends, James Cyril Puttington. Not only is Puttie the complete gentleman, he is also the most unselfish, considerate and honest chap I've had the good fortune to meet. I'll go further and say that he is the only person in the world, outside my close family, to whom I would hand over my wife, kids, house and box for temporary custody without any qualms as to their safe return.

Puttie must be about ten years my senior and therefore, I have never seen him at the height of his powers as a sportsman. He went to a top public school where he became captain of cricket and fives and was also a more than useful rugger player. Though quite recently married, over most of the time I've known him he has been the confirmed batchelor, diligent at his job and holding numerous posts as secretary, organiser and dedicated supporter of various clubs, who may or may not have appreciated his services.

Puttie has a magnificent sense of humour and plays the comic rôle of the pedantic accident-prone gentleman by second nature. In addition, his schooling normally prevents the spontaneous expression of abuse, let alone slang or blasphemies. This point is always born uppermost in mind by his relatively uncouth team-mates, delighted to hear his rare outbursts of anger prefaced with—'Bother me, with respect, may I be allowed to suggest that . . . etc., etc.'

Short, thick set and very strong, as befits an officer and gentleman, Puttie is completely fearless physically, almost to the point of fool-hardiness. His cry: 'Come with me Brighton', is well known to local rugger enthusiasts and I had the good fortune to witness it's use before I got to know him well.

Standing on the touchline at Withdean Stadium one day, I was watching the Brighton 'A' team take a hammering from a London side with Puttie performing defensive miracles at full-back, tackling single-handed and head-on all over the field. The opposition were awarded a penalty about thirty yards out from the posts and a poor attempt at goal was fielded by Puttie half-way from the corner flag. Without hesitation he set off down the field, ball clutched under arm, chin up, his short legs going like pistons and crying: 'Come with me Brighton, come with me!'

No-one did, of course, and as he approached the solid wall of human flesh, I winced and was forced to avert my gaze to avoid a sickening spectacle of blood and smashed bones. When I found the courage to look back, the ball was emerging from a heap of opposition players with Puttie underneath—I would think just below ground level. When the last body had rolled off, Puttie remained inert for a few seconds, then picked himself up slowly as stud marks became visible on every inch of exposed flesh. Eventually he trotted back gingerly to his position and resumed his heroics.

Puttie moved down to Brighton from the Croydon area around 1960, and played cricket for Rottingdean before joining St. James's. The circumstances of our introduction, in his first match for the club, are worthy of recall. Fielding first in a game at Stanmer Park, I was posted to backward short-leg where I noticed the newcomer in multi-coloured cap, positioned alongside, set for action in aggressive and determined style. The opening bat pushed forward to the first few balls and then latched on to a short one and slammed it down to fine-leg with great aplomb. Without moving, I swivelled round to watch the ball bounce a couple of times before crossing the boundary but was then surprised to feel a thump on the ground in front of me. Turning back I looked down to see Puttie spreadeagled on the turf, arms outstretched, presumably at the end of his attempt to cut off the shot. He rolled over, looked up and said:

'Bother me, I was a bit late on that one, old chap. I don't believe we've met, my name is James Puttington.'

He then proffered his hand vertically upwards and we exchanged the normal pleasantries from this unusual position.

Having only seen Puttie perform in the more domestic rôle, I've rarely watched him in full flow, but he has played some invaluable defensive innings. With a distinctive style, crouching low at the crease, cap perched at a determined angle, he has a tremendous back-lift which means that he is often castled if the ball keeps low. With a solid defensive push he is also an expert leaver of the ball outside the off-stump. To anything short in this region, he jumps across with both feet and crouches down, bat over shoulder, hoping the ball will pass harmlessly overhead. The theory, of course, is excellent, but the practice tends to be a trifle painful, especially on a soft slow wicket.

Puttie carries his kit in an enormous brown initialled suitcase and as a pipe smoker of the clenched teeth variety, is always well equipped with tobacco, cleaning rods, lighter fuel, etc., mixed up with soap, jock straps and talcum powder. For some reason I took a closer look at his kit one day, and noticed in the corner of his case a peculiarly shaped key which obviously couldn't be used for any normal household purpose. When I tackled him about it, he explained in great detail that it was a special key to release the emergency safety harness on certain military aircraft. This is typical of his consideration for others, and incredibly useful; so if you should stumble across a crashed Lightning Jet fighter pilot, manfully struggling to release the safety harness before becoming enveloped in flames, please do not hesitate to give Puttie a ring—preferably during the cricket season.

Puttie is one of those accident-prone individuals, always embroiled in some misfortune or other. A typical example of this was when he arrived half-an-hour late for a match at Horley one year, and rushed into the changing room apologizing profusely. He went on to explain that he had rolled his car over on the A23, and had had to get a hand in righting it before continuing his journey. We were stunned at this, picturing him as the lone survivor of a horrific motorway type multi-car pile-up but it turned out that he had only misjudged his speed at the entrance to a petrol station. I trust the garage had the decency to give him bonus stamps for enthusiasm!

On the field of play he tends to be the heroic fielder who saves four over-throws with his shins while backing-up, and he's also established a world batting record by managing to be struck painfully on the hand or fingers to all six balls in one particular over.

On this theme, I recall a Puttie incident at Ashurst Wood a few years back, when we were put into bat on a fiery track and the stars got out, or got themselves out, pretty smartly. Puttie went to the crease and commenced a valiant rear-guard action and only came undone when he tried to take the initiative. Swinging violently at a fast short-pitched ball he missed it, and was hit smack on the right eye, felling him instantly. He had caught a real pearler, and as everybody rushed up to the wicket in genuine concern, he was writhing in agony, emitting many ow's, ooch's and aarrr's. We gathered round in the usual helpless way and after he'd got over the worst of the trauma, his first words were, 'Bother me, I'm dreadfully sorry about this, I shouldn't be holding up the game. Please carry on without me.' The thought did cross my mind that it would be a trifle difficult to continue with him lying across the crease, but Puttie continued his abject apologies, eye visibly closing and looking the most horrible mess. Finally he was helped off and someone ran him to the hospital where he had to stay the night for observation. I understand he was still apologizing when the skipper went to visit him later that evening but mercifully he made a full recovery with his reputation for unselfishness in action greatly enhanced.

Puttie and barbed wire seem to have a mutual attraction, and Pickering and Boyd-Pain played a typically loutish schoolboy trick on him one year at Firle. It's a superb setting with the pitch in a secluded park within a stone's throw of the pub and cut off from the main stream of people and traffic. We've played there for a number of years now, and the pitch for our first fixture was what I had best tactfully described as 'unpredict-able.' In practical terms this meant that the star batsmen, big-heartedly agreed to let the domestics have a go further up the order, whilst the star bowlers paced out their run-ups before the match started.

The incident occurred when we were in the field after tea and one of their batsmen, sleeves rolled above thick bronzed fore-arms, was unable to spot a cleverly flighted leg-break, and deposited the ball deep into the woods at the bottom end of the ground. Puttie, stationed at deep long-on, managed to negotiate the barbed wire fence and disappeared into the wood to retrieve. After a few seconds he reappeared at the other side and lobbed the ball back onto the pitch. As he started to squirm his way under the bottom wire, Pickering and Boyd-Pain intervened by shouting frantically, 'Wait Puttie!, you're trapped, don't move.' They then crept back to their fielding positions and two more balls were bowled, with Puttie lying face downwards in the mud under the fence hopefully waiting assistance. When he finally realized he had been conned he trotted, seething, back onto the field and unleashed a stream of vitriolic abuse at the offenders starting with, 'Bother me, chaps. With respect, I don't feel that that sort of joke is really on.'

St. James's would probably elect as their favourite Puttie story the course of events which took place in the Hailsham match of 1965. It was a hot August Sunday which poets describe with much use of the words 'idyllic', 'azure', and 'languid'. The star batsmen were almost coming to blows over the order, but I was pleased when we batted first, and as a domestic was able to slump into a deck-chair and let it all happen. We had a chap called Tim Redman playing for us at that time who was in the super-star category (Somerset 2nd XI), and he opened the innings and started pushing the ball around the park with nonchalant ease. I must have nodded off because I was awakened by thunderous applause when he reached his ton and we declared soon after with about 220 for 3. With too many sandwiches and cream doughnuts under the belt, we took the field, confident that the opposition wouldn't be able to match our score, al-though not so certain about getting them out.

The opening bowlers pushed them behind the clock and with about 150 required in the last hour, the skipper decided on aerial assault and Norman Wilson was brought on to fire off some 'Bazooka' leg breaks from the bottom end. We posted our-selves round the boundary at thirty yard intervals and with Puttie positioned at long-on, Wilson delivered three balls which resulted in the following sequence of events.

The first ball, designed to turn in behind the batsman was

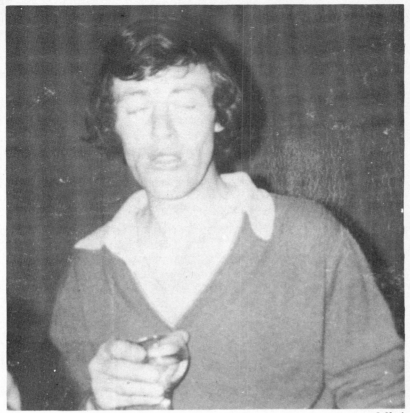

Derek J. Pickering, Captain of St. James's C.C., 1963–65, 1970—

A classic tour portrait of our revered skipper as he nears the end of a very long evening

struck powerfully towards mid-off and when it was about two hundred feet above ground level and still rising, Puttie sprinted off from his position with a spectacular catch in mind. Before he could reach the flight path, he had to negotiate the front of the sight screen and he overlooked the presence of some sturdy guy ropes holding it in position. He executed three or four perfect cartwheels in a balletic slow motion, before coming to rest in a crumpled heap as the ball, still rising, disappeared over the trees at least 30 yards behind the boundary.

Ball number two, a cleverly disguised 'googly' was misread by the batsman who despatched it with frightening force, this time passing over Puttie's head into the woods behind. Puttie successfully negotiated the barbed wire fence as at Firle, and lobbed the ball back onto the field where it was returned to the bowler. As Norman Wilson was about to run in for his next ball, the batsman stood up and pointed towards Puttie, and we looked round to find him hopelessly embroiled in barbed wire, struggling like a demented Houdini. He was eventually given assistance by a fielder explicitly instructed to do so by the skipper, and he returned to the fray, apologising passionately for delaying the game and assuring the opposition that he would make any financial reparations necessary for damage caused to the fence.

The third ball, bowled with over-spin and flatter trajectory to hurry through off the track was again struck to a great height, towards Puttie at deep mid-on. This time from the moment of contact, and in spite of many directional changes caused by turbulence in the jet stream, Puttie did not move a muscle and remained crouched, legs apart, apparently transfixed as the ball homed down into his hands like a guided missile. He held the catch perfectly, and we all threw caps in the air, and rushed up in delight to congratulate him while he insisted modestly that all credit was due to Wilson's skilful bowling.

Anyone as unselfish as Puttie automatically gets put upon by less talented and civilised individuals and I remember a series of incidents during and after a match at Maresfield one Sunday. As we had to field first, we all went into the changing room at more or less the same time, including a chap called David Trencham who, although a pretty domestic cricketer, was a big hairy rugger player of some repute. Somehow or other, Trencham's cricket kit had got mixed up the day before and he only realized as he opened his bag that the gear belonged to a certain Adrian Shillaker, who was not playing in this particular match. After he emitted the usual mouthful of swear words, a strange quiet came over the changing room as one or two rapid calculations were made. Adrian Shillaker was a very slim chap, about a quarter the diameter of Trencham, and in addition a snappy dresser, rather inclined to tapered trouser legs with seven inch bottoms, etc. While most of us cottoned on to the potential dangers of this situation, Puttie sucked happily away at his pipe and started changing in his methodical manner, whilst the rest of us surreptitiously speeded up our changing process to get out onto the field as quickly as possible.

68

With only Trencham and Puttie left inside, I don't really want to know exactly what happened, but the first things to emerge were the hairy legs of Trencham as he stomped onto the pitch like a gorilla in Bermuda shorts. With bated breath, we awaited the emergence of Puttie, who eventually appeared looking cross and flustered, and minced uncomfortably onto the pitch with his appearance below the waist best described as something between Lester Piggot and Rudolph Nureyev.

I remember that match particularly because a strange thing happened just after tea as we stood around outside the pavilion chucking a few balls at the openers before the game re-started. From the pavilion at Maresfield you can look out across the countryside to the west part of the town, and two or three players were taking in the view, when somebody casually pointed out a pall of smoke about a quarter of a mile away. Suddenly one of their players shouted, 'Good grief, that's my house'. He tore off up the drive in full cricket gear and was not to be seen again. Without wishing to be too unsympathetic, I can't remember whether we offered them a sub or not.

I believe we won the game, but in any event everyone was in high spirits in the changing room afterwards and Puttie joined in the fun by going into the shower, naked naturally, but with pipe clenched firmly between teeth, bowl upside-down to prevent the water from dousing the flames. This went down very well of course, but after a couple of minutes there was a piercing shriek and when I poked my head round the door, Puttie was doubled up, pipe in the gulley, while he seemed to be executing some sort of war dance. Without further explanation you will have deduced that a piece of red hot ash had fallen from his pipe onto an ultra-sensitive part of his anatomy!

We moved on to the Chequers for the evening session, which continued till closing time before we set off back to Brighton. As we had not eaten properly all day, we decided to stop on the way at a Chinese restaurant in Lewes for a quick meal. Seven of us led by Puttie trooped in, where we were escorted to a long table in the corner. Puttie is a self-confessed expert in oriental cuisine and he stated confidently that the numbering system on the menu is universal to all Chinese restaurants, and he kept a list of excellent dishes in his diary. Too hungry to argue, we left him to get on with it but took a dim view when we were eventually served with four different types of rice, plus plain egg foo-yong, curried egg foo-yong and spiced egg foo-yong.

Each dish was placed at the end of the table and passed down from man to man, and at that time of night it's not easy to deal out precisely one seventh from an oval shaped bowl being pulled away from you by the chap next in line. The first man tended to err towards a quarter, the second perhaps a fifth, and so on. When we were ready for the 'off', I glanced along the line and noticed that the first man had a massive mound of food spilling onto the tablecloth whereas Puttie at the other end had exactly twenty-four grains of rice, seven bamboo shoots and three peas. I commented tentatively on this disparity, to which came his immediate reply: 'Quite all right old boy; I wasn't very hungry anyway'. To add insult to injury, when it came to squaring up the bill, one chap declared he was a bit short and had to ask Puttie for a loan to pay his share.

As we left, Puttie was still sorting out what gratuity to leave and busy sending complimentary messages to the chef, and I couldn't help reflecting that with politicians trying to phase out public schools, people like Puttie are, metaphorically speaking, a dying race. This is a great loss as I would love the opportunity to witness the reaction of Dennis Lillee, having pinged his third bouncer past the tailender's nose, to be greeted with: 'Bother me bowler, with respect, this sort of thing's not really on'.

P.S.—As most of this chapter was a ruthless exposure of Puttie's misfortunes on and off the field of play, I was faced with the delicate problem of obtaining his approval before going into print. Having conjured up many devious schemes to get him sloshed so that he would agree to anything, I took the coward's way out in the end, wrapped the copy in plain brown paper and slipped it in the post. His courteous reply, fulsome with praise, politely pointed out some spelling mistakes and loose grammar, but indicated that for the price of a couple of jars I could go ahead.

8. My Star Performances

This chapter will, by necessity, be very long as there are so many star performances in my hundreds of trips to the wickets over the years. It may be easier, in fact, to produce a separate volume, probably in several parts, listing the fullest details in order to satisfy all my fans, hungry for statistics, and ball by ball commentary. Until such time as I can prepare this volume I hope the reader will be satisfied with a fairly short catalogue of my greatest innings.

Having said all that, it is extremely difficult to know where to start. One's mind drifts back over the many scintillating fifties stroked effortlessly in double quick time, when the going was good. Then there's the brutal and extrovert canings meted out to star bowlers who had had the temerity to remove my colleagues from the firing line. Again, there's the desecration and humiliation of sub-standard offerings from domestic bowlers, struggling to make their minuscule mark on the game. And of course there's always those tenacious backs-to-the-wall dogfights on an unplayable track in near darkness in order to save the side.

One can always dream! !

J. Wensley

A pathetic attempt to pressurise the author when in full flow (where the ball went is a mere detail).

9. Christmas Day

Every year around ten o'clock in the morning on Christmas Day a cricket match gets under way at Preston Park, Brighton. The origins of the match are of some interest and I am indebted to Noel Bennett, a popular character in local circles, who filled me in with much of the detail. It would perhaps be unfair to add that this information was obtained with the aid of a string of 'baby Stingo's', on which Noel is a national expert.

When World War II started, Noel was playing for Brighton Electricity and although Adolf had the courtesy to wait until the end of the 1939 season before starting hostilities, he rather disturbed the club cricket circuit in 1940. With most club cricketers pressed into uniform only a few teams managed to keep going and as a result, Brighton Electricity were obliged to play St. Mary's (one of the oldest local clubs), no less than six times. It was a fine summer, weatherwise, and the last fixture held early in October resulted in the two teams being level in the rubber, so the captains agreed to play a decider on Christmas Day.

Thus established, the match has been held every year since, although the teams are now called Noel Bennett's XI and the Yulelogs. The game has only been cancelled or abandoned in the face of persistent rain, and is played as a serious competitive match limited to about twenty overs a side.

I played for the Yulelogs for seven or eight years in the sixties, and naturally there have been a number of amusing incidents apart from the fact that special batting and bowling techniques are required.

Some sort of record may have been established one year when, with the pitch a mud bath after incessant rain throughout December, there were no less than seven run-outs during one innings. It was not so much that batsmen were unable to turn, but more that they were unable to move, and hitting fours was the only effective way of scoring runs. Even that was easier said than done, as the sheer momentum of swinging the bat could be enough to loosen the foothold.

N. Bennett's XI *v.* Yulelogs, Christmas Day, 1964

(The author is in this picture, completely obscured of course!)

I might add that my own performances in some of these matches were almost of star quality which I can only put down to my normal batting style, best described as having no back-lift, too much right hand and a complete absence of foot-work. This 'style' is well-suited to batting in a quagmire, with the ball skidding through at ankle height, and I am proud of the occasion I scored 20 out of a score of 40 all out, in a match we won by 2 runs. What's more, due to over-enthusiasm by the team secretaries, we played twelve a side.

On another year we had heavy snow so the start was held up for a few minutes, as it was felt prudent to sweep off the wicket at least, before getting underway. I was well prepared for the game, wearing two pairs of pyjamas under shirt and flannels, with as many sweaters as I could lay my hands on piled on top. This enabled me to keep reasonably warm while in the field, apart from a mild attack of frost-bite on the extremities. Standing at deep long-on for most of the match, one powerfully struck drive ended up as a stationary snowball at my feet, and they crossed for another run, while I sorted the ball out.

The great Peter Beecheno played for Bennett's XI for many years and I always felt he demonstrated his real star quality on these occasions. He would arrive straight from bed, slightly hung over, from a heavy Christmas Eve session, not having seen a cricket ball for several months. Invariably he would open the bowling and having struggled bleerily up the wicket, the first ball would be bang on a length, or as he would say, 'there or there-abouts'.

Naturally Beech was involved in creating some fine incidents, like the year a television crew came along to get a few shots of the game. Due to the programme schedule they couldn't wait for the proper match to begin, so the stumps were put out, someone padded up and Beech went out to throw down a few balls while the cameraman took some close-ups of the batsman. Anxious for a shot of the batsman being bowled, the cameraman asked Beech to oblige, from half-way down the wicket. Blinking heavily, Beech couldn't hit the stumps, and moved in to only three yards away before he managed to hit the woodwork. Soon after that, the match proper started and Beech happened to be bowling to the same batsman. He bowled him first ball!

Another year we had had a dry but bitterly cold December, and consequently after a heavy frost the pitch was frozen, bone hard. The umpires went out to put in the stumps but couldn't make any impression at all and they retired while a mallet was found. For ten minutes they sweated away with the echo ringing round the ground, before they succeeded in driving in the stumps.

Noel Bennett and the opposing captain, Ted Wigglesworth, went out to toss up and Beech, as usual, went along to inspect the track. Noel called correctly but before announcing his decision noticed Beech looking at the wicket with a big grin. After a succession of chortles he called out, 'Put 'em in Noel, put 'em in.'

As on many previous occasions, Noel did as requested, and a few minutes later Beech, raring to go, was in action from the top end. The reason for his enthusiasm soon became clear; he had spotted some frozen worm casts just about on a length and pitching bang on, the ball reared up and ricochetted about in all directions as batsmen groped forward like blind men.

To return to Noel Bennett, few cricketers could have a more impeccable pedigree. He is rightly proud of the fact that his great-great-great-grandfather was John Small, one of the stars of the Hambledonians XI which played All England in the late eighteenth century. John Small was, I believe, the chap who batted for three days for very few runs and come to think of it Noel seems to have inherited his defensive talents, as to my knowledge he rarely played a stroke in anger.

Noel is a short, bespectacled, rotund figure with a distinctive waddling gait, and as he is thirty years my senior I've never seen him in his cricketing prime.

Before he stopped playing a few years back, I did play against him and remember him as the slowest bowler I've faced, though by no means the least effective. Tossing the ball yards into the air off a 'shuffle-up' of about four feet, my first reaction, as a rash intemperate youth, was to decide that he had to be hit out of the ground. I was deflated and peeved to be left stranded half-way down the wicket watching the ball bounce several times before gently tapping the stumps.

Most coaching manuals, incidentally, are deliberately vague on how to cope with the ball dropping vertically out of the sky. If you attempt to get your head over the ball, apart from the risk of getting hit in the back of the neck, there's always the chance of being caught off the end of the bat handle. So, the only options are to play across the line, or hit it back, 'from whence it came', with all the attendant dangers.

As the founder and skipper of Noel Bennett's XI, Noel is the

75

only player to have played in every Christmas Day game to date, and I still cherish the memory of the match with thick snow on the ground. Fortified by a nip of whisky, the deadly serious Noel waddled out from the pavilion with the opposing skipper to inspect the wicket—if they could find it! ! !

10. The Changing Room

One part of the club cricket ritual which I particularly enjoy is sampling the buoyant repartee and subtle wit which often takes place in the changing room before a match. Fortunately St. James's C.C. have usually had a number of extrovert characters to make this all the more entertaining and I relate below the typical exchanges prior to a match (with apologies to David Storey). In addition I hope to demonstrate the smooth, efficient organisation of a crack side as the players key themselves up for a vital match.

Arriving at the ground at 2.20, perhaps rather late for a 2.30 start, I enter the changing room to find just four players assembled, Hunt (Team Secretary), Gaskell, Withers and DaVall. After the usual greetings, and anxious to find out what happened last Sunday, when I was not playing, the chat proceeds as follows:

Me What happened last Sunday?

Hunt Oh we stuffed 'em. We batted first and creamed 170 odd, and then they struggled and were all out for around 100.

Me Marvellous, who did what? I suppose Watkins got all the runs?

Hunt No, I think he got a blonger actually. Everyone got a few, you know.

DaVall Watkins did not star, but one or two of the domestics made some useful contributions.

Me Meaning you of course.

DaVall Well modesty forbade me to spell it out, but since you're pressing me, I did stroke a rather elegant 27.

Withers Well, if we're going to blow our own trumpets, I'd like to refer to a certain penetrative spell of hostile medium-pace bowling in adverse conditions . . .

76

Me All right, all right, I've got the drift. So our so-called stars failed to perform.

Hunt Gask got 5 wickets.

Me Mmmmm ... must have been 5 for plenty. I trust you purchased a jug, Gask?

Gask Well ... er ... um ... what happened was ...

Me Oh, that's all right, Gask. If you forgot, I'll make sure you don't go tonight without squaring up.

(*Door opens and Pickering (skipper), Sam and Nick enter with the usual, 'hallo chaps', etc., etc. Sam looks ashen-faced and haggard, and mumbling a few words, dumps his kit and sprawls out on a bench in the corner.*)

Me What happened to Sam? He looks disgusting.

Nick Oh, he had a very heavy night, big bird, very demanding. He'll be all right by tea.

Pick Well that's not much good, I'm expecting him to bowl this afternoon.

Me Well surely we can't be that desperate!

Withers Thank you very much chaps, your confidence in the bowling is much appreciated.

Hunt What we doing, Skip?

Pick Well give me a chance, I only just got here.

(*Much commotion as door opens and in walks Puttie, complete with pipe and large suitcase.*)

Puttie Gentlemen, I'm extremely sorry I'm late, will you please accept my apologies?

Chorus No.

Puttie Derek, I'm sorry, I seem to have mislaid my box. Very remiss of me.

Pick That's quite all right, James. Now then come on everybody, I want you ready in two minutes.

Nick Hey, you should have seen Boyd-Pain last week. He was pathetic. Sweetman had been tossing up his leggers all afternoon, and their chap had been striking them out of the ground, and the first one he mis-hits goes straight to B.P. who doesn't want to know. He just did not want to know, pretending the sun was in his eyes ! ! ! !

Me Well, you can't have everything. B.P.'s got all the talents known to man, but they can be a bit of a liability.

Nick As far as I'm concerned, Boyd-Pain is an absolute ...

(*Crash! Door opens and in walks B.P. to be greeted by general abuse.*)

77

J. Hindmarsh

Tony DaVall's boots

Radio-carbon dating suggests conception circa 1937

B.P. Sorry skip, traffic was dreadful, got stuck behind some old
girl driving right in the middle of the road she was, doing
exactly ten miles an hour, I never saw anything . . .
Pick All right, all right we've heard all that before, just hurry up
and get on with it.
B.P. What we doing then, Skip?
Pick I don't know yet.
B.P. Hey chaps, I heard a tremendous story this week. It's about
a coloured bloke on a building site. Have you heard it?
Me Yes, quite definitely.
B.P. Anyone else heard it?
Withers As there are, at a conservative estimate, about a million
jokes concerning coloured blokes on building sites, I'm
prepared to say that there is a fair chance that I haven't heard it.
B.P. Right, O.K. then. Well you see there's this coloured bloke
looking for a job on a building site . . .

78

(Door opens, and the opposing skipper pokes his head in, and enquires whether our skipper is ready to go out and toss up. Pickering says he'll be right with him. At the same time I notice DaVall about to put on his boots).

Me Those boots, DaVall, must be the perfect domestic model; just one eye-hole and two studs and they've certainly never been cleaned for years. Magnificent ! ! !

DaVall I resent the implication that my apparel is not what it might be. The boots you are looking at have, in fact, two eye-holes, three studs, one of which was put in as recently as two years ago.

Me O.K. O.K. but they are perfect buckskin, completely un-cleaned, they must be fifteen years old?

DaVall I would say more like twenty years.

(At this point Withers throws one of his boots onto the table in the middle of the changing room.)

Withers How's that then for a pure domestic boot?

Puttie I must say, gentlemen, with respect, that any self-respecting cricketer is extremely particular about his appearance and . . .

Me Trouble is, Puttie, we haven't got any self-respecting cricketers.

(As I examine Withers' boot, Sam emits a low moan from his position on the bench.)

Pick What's wrong with Sam?

Nick Don't worry about it. It's just some sort of delayed ecstasy from last night.

Withers I must say, I don't know whether all this drink and fornication is worth the effort, if that's what it reduces you to.

Me Withers, this boot is a perfect example of crumpled canvas, hanging limply on a platform of rotten leather, and there must be one knot per inch. Absolutely superb.

Withers Well, I think they've seen better days, but I've decided that they'll pack up when I do, or vice-versa.

B.P. Hey, do you want to hear the rest of this story about the coloured chap . . .

(General chorus of 'Get on with it Boyd-Pain'.)

B.P. Well there was this coloured bloke you see, and he's looking for a job, so he goes off to this building site and he goes up to the foreman, and he says, 'Boss have you got a job for a . . . errr . . . , you know the er . . . bloke that carries the bricks up the ladder.'

DaVall A hod-carrier's mate.

B.P. Yeah, that's right, a hod-carrier's mate. Anyway the foreman bloke says, 'O.K. we need one of them, you can start right away, but first, what's your name?'

(*Hunt looking out of the window watches Pickering tossing up with the opposing skipper.*)

Hunt Skipper's just tossed up.

Me Let me know what we're doing, otherwise I'll have got my boots on, perhaps unnecessarily.

Hunt Ha! Ha! Ha! Very funny, Pickering.

Nick What's that?

Hunt Pickering's just made a funny, he bowled his arm over to indicate we were fielding, then immediately tapped both knees to indicate we were batting.

DaVall That's just about the limit of Pickering's sense of humour.

Nick Incorrect; he cribbed it from their skipper last week (*general laughter*).

B.P. Anyway, before I was so rudely interrupted, this coloured bloke says to the foreman, he says, 'Boss,' he says, 'My name is Mick.' And the foreman says, 'Well we can't call you that, because we've already got a chap called Mick, so we'll call you wog,' 'Wog! !,' he says, 'Wog—you can't call me Wog, I'll go down the relations . . .'—Whatsit—the race ouja, what's the name of the people?'

Me The Race Relations Board.

Nick Get on with it, B.P.

B.P. Yeah, O.K. the Race Relations Board then. Er . . . where was I?

Me Our coloured colleague was just about to make representations to the . . .

B.P. Oh yeah, so the foreman says, 'You can go where you like, old sport, but as far as I'm concerned, if you want this job we're calling you Wog.' So the coloured bloke thinks to himself, I need this job badly, I need the money, so I'll have to say yes. So he says, 'O.K. boss, you can call me Wog.'

(*B.P. is interrupted by Gaskell, who suddenly erupts with an explosion of blasphemies.*)

Me What's wrong, Gask?

Gask She's done it again, she's left out me shirt. You'd never believe it. Anyone got a spare shirt?

(*Chorus No, sorry, Gask, etc., etc.*)

DaVall There may be a spare umpire's coat in the club kit, Gask. You could always tuck the tails down your trouser legs.

Gask Ha! Ha! Very funny.

Me I think you ought to go to the wicket, Gask, just wearing two sweaters and rip them off fiercely at the beginning of the first over. I think that would strike terror in the hearts of the opposing batters. (Laughter).

Gask All this is very funny, but someone's got to find me a shirt.

Puttie You could always borrow mine if we're batting first, Peter.

B.P. Anyway the foreman he er . . .

DaVall Come on B.P., I thought you'd finished.

B.P. Hang about. This foreman, he says to Wog, 'Right Wog, come along here and I'll introduce you to your mates.' So he takes him down to the hut to two or three blokes sitting there having tea, and he says, 'Here's a new man and he's called Wog,' he says, 'Now this is Paddy, he's from Ireland, this is Mac, from Scotland, this is Jack, who's a cockney, and this is Mick from Liverpool.' 'Right,' he says, 'Now everyone knows everyone, get on with it.'

(Door opens and Pickering returns from the wicket to be greeted by chorus of, 'what we doing then, skip'?)

Pick Gentlemen you will be pleased to know that we are in the field. (*Uproar, with cries of 'Oh no', 'Not again'; 'Surely not'; 'Pickering is useless', etc., etc.*)

Me How many times have we won the toss this season?

Pick How do you know I lost the toss today?

Withers Well, if you won the toss and put them in with a thunderstorm imminent, I feel we shall have to call a committee meeting to discuss the captaincy.

Nick Good idea, let's make it The Star of Brunswick on Tuesday.

Pick All right lads, let's cut out the banter. Now let me see, we've got eleven players. Umpire? . . . Hunt, have we got an umpire?

Hunt Yes, Bert Amor is making his own way here.

Pick Good . . . What about a scorer?

Hunt No, Morgan can't do it today.

Pick O.K. then, right chaps, pull yourselves together and let's see you out on the field in two minutes.

Me Thought about a wicket-keeper, skip?

Pick Good point, J.L.H. is not playing . . . I suppose you'll have to keep, Dick.

Me Thank you very much, the last resort as usual. Where's the club kit?

Pick Good point again. Who's got the club kit?

Hunt I thought you were bringing it.

Pick I haven't seen it. Where were we playing last week?

Withers Horley, Nick and I distinctly remember Sweetman loading the kit into his car.

Nick That's right I remember, I couldn't take it, and he volunteered.

Pick Good, that's settled then. Sweetman's got the club kit, now then come on everybody, let's see some action.

Hunt There's only one snag.

Pick What's that?

Hunt Sweetman's not playing!

Pick Good God, you are an absolute shower. Look, who is playing? Stand still everybody while I have a count up . . . One, two, three, four, five, six, seven, eight, nine, ten. Now who's missing?

Davall Pickering showing off his education again. Not a moment's hesitation between those numbers.

Hunt Watkins.

Me A typical star. Always late . . .

Pick Look, Dick, you'll have to ask their keeper if you can borrow his gloves.

Withers Boyd-Pain, I'm still trying to work out whether we've reached the punch line in your joke. If we have, I'm delighted to say that I've forgotten it already.

B.P. Oh yes . . . yes my joke, um . . . where'd I got to?

Nick He'd just introduced him to his mates.

B.P. Oh yes that's right he um . . ., well he goes off to work and at the end of the week it's pay-day and he goes up to the boss and he says, 'Boss where's my pay?' The foreman says . . . he says, 'Er . . . sorry, Wog, no pay for you this week, the company only pays every fortnight'. So Wog says, 'You can't do that. I must have my money. I've got a wife and fourteen kids to support, I'll starve, this is terrible, you've got to pay me.' (*Puttie has just lit up his pipe again, dense clouds of smoke are now filling the changing room. B.P. starts choking . . .*)

B.P. Good grief, Puttie, what on earth's in that pipe?

Puttie It's a ready-rubbed mixture of seaweed and old jock-straps actually, old boy.

B.P. Well, for goodness sake douse the flames somebody.

Me O.K. I'll fetch a bucket of water.

Puttie: I'm dreadfully sorry, old boy, I should have realised that it's an acquired taste. I'll put it out immediately.

Me Right, get on with it B.P. 'A wife and fourteen kids . . .'

B.P. Oh yes, that's right, a wife and fourteen kids um . . . So the foreman says, 'I'm sorry, but er . . . that's the company rule, there's nothing I can do about it.' So Wog says, 'Well look, boss,' he says, 'If you can't pay me, how about giving me a sub, just a few quid so that I can buy some food for the kids.' So the foreman says, 'I'll tell you what I'll do, we'll call a meeting and we'll have a whip round if the lads agree.' So Wog says, 'O.K. boss.'

DaVall I sense that we might be within five minutes or so of the punch line.

B.P. Quiet, just listen will you. Anyway so they call a meeting and . . .

Pick Is Sam alright?

Hunt I think he's dead, actually.

Pick Well give him a prod will you, and tell him to get on with it.

B.P. Anyway, as I was saying, they have this meeting and the boss says, wait for it chaps, now here it comes, the boss says, 'Right, Mick, Mac, Paddy, Jack, give a wog a loan.'
(*Uproar! Boots, shoes, cricket kit, etc. are hurled at B.P. who cowers in a corner with a delighted smirk on his face. Around this time Watkins, the last man, slips into the room unnoticed and starts changing quickly.*)

Puttie With respect old boy, I must say I feel that that joke is in rather poor taste.

Hunt I wouldn't even classify it as a joke.

Pick Thank goodness that's over with. Can I have everybody on the field immediately please?
(*Players start to troop out as Bert Amor (umpire) walks in.*)

Bert Terribly sorry I'm late Derek, the traffic was terrible, I got stuck behind a chap who couldn't have been doing much more than ten miles an hour . . .

Pick Oh, I know it's terrible Bert, never mind. Look! We're in the field, are you all set?

Bert Yes. O.K. Derek I'm all ready, but there's one snag. My wife washed my umpire's coat and unfortunately she didn't have time to iron it, have we got a spare?

Pick Oh, yes that's all right Bert, there a spare one in the club kit.
(*Pause*) Oh . . . * * * * * . . . ! ! ! ! !
Play ! !

11. *Women*

I've never been much of a womaniser and even if I were, the fact that my wife is typing these details places certain limits on what can be said. When I first started playing club cricket, any wives or girl-friends who did come along to a match tended to be parked in deck-chairs and allowed to brown off, or get browned off during the course of the game. Similarly, once in the pub after the match, they would be fed the odd gin and tonic and left to get on with their own small talk, while us males discussed much weightier topics, such as whether their umpire was bent or simply incompetent.

I suppose it is to the credit of 'Women's Lib' that things are much more equal and free and easy these days, but the woman who can down a couple of pints while debating the finer points of the l.b.w. law is still a rare bird.

First dates, romance and marriage pose a delicate situation to the ardent club cricketer. I've seen many a blossoming friendship wither and die on the tricky problems of how much cricket he was intending to play, and what she was supposed to do in the meantime. Similarly of course, marriages break up with the strain this can cause, but perhaps the saddest situation is to watch a talented young player being allowed only one game a fortnight by his girl-friend or spouse, and thereby loose form and subsequently, interest in the game.

I can justifiably claim to have handled my own courtship and marriage with consummate skill in this direction. Carol and I had our first date in December one year at the annual rugger club ball and as I rapidly became inebriated, it is difficult to believe I made a favourable impression. I can only conclude that she was able to perceive nobler qualities beneath my bleary eyes and incoherent patter. Being the close season, I had no reason to mention cricket and our relationship blossomed until, at the beginning of April, I suddenly realised that the new season started in a few weeks' time, and that I hadn't as yet broached the subject.

One of the first things which attracted me to Carol was the fact that at the time she drank halves of bitter, although of course once I became hooked, she moved on to more exotic pastures. One April evening, therefore, I plied her with halves in our local, and then popped the dreaded question.

'What do you think about cricket'?

Her honest but shattering reply was:

'Cricket? ? ! ! ! I've never seen a game in my life ! ! !'

Managing to hide my dismay, I launched into a sales patter about it being part of our heritage, with lazy picnics in the countryside under hot summer skies, followed by refreshment and convivial chat in the local hostelry. This idyllic picture did not quite materialise for the first match of the season against Keymer and Hassocks at the end of April. It was, in fact, a cold and miserable day with the ground sodden underfoot and the heavens poised to open up at any time. Carol dutifully came along, and I parked her in a deck-chair near the club-house, swathed in spare clothing, and pointed her mummified figure in the general direction of the wicket. At the interval, I poured much steaming hot tea down her throat in an attempt to raise the body temperature and delay the onset of rigor mortis. After stumps were drawn, I changed quickly and rushed into the club-house, which fortunately incorporated a bar, and said in an enthusiastic and businesslike tone:—

'Now then, my dear, what would you like? A double scotch?'

This was a good first move and for an hour or so several of us chatted her up fiercely while plying her with drinks at a frenzied rate. Surreptitiously, I then slid into the conversation the apparently casual question:—

'What do you think of cricket?'

By this time she was bubbling merrily and answered quite freely that she thought it was interesting and that she wouldn't mind coming along next week if she had nothing else to do. A potential crisis in our relationship was thus avoided by skilful teamwork and some worthwhile additional expense.

From this modest start grew great things, and by the end of the season Carol was a competent scorer, knew what l.b.w. meant and could prepare twenty-six teas by five o'clock. I can look back with some pride, therefore, at the masterly way I enlightened her pitiful ignorance of the game, a view nowadays she does not always share when faced with a pile of dirty trousers and smelly jock-straps on a Monday morning.

The wife enthralled by her first ever cricket match at Keymer and Hassocks, April 1967

It was decided by the Committee, during a heavy session in the Cricketers at Broadwater Green, that Carol was the right girl for me.

I therefore plucked up courage and popped the ultimate question standing outside the Pavilion Hotel in Brighton in June of that year. To this day there is a rumbling domestic dispute over this uninteresting piece of personal history, as I claim that I must have been drunk to have popped the question, and therefore we were on our way out. Conversely, she claims that to have made such a humble, eloquent and impassioned plea for her hand, I must have been sober and therefore we were on our way into the pub. Anyway, having received the affirmative, we certainly went back inside to soothe my nerves and, emboldened by my success, I went on to explain tactfully that the wedding would, of course, have to take place in the close season.

Our wedding day was in January of the next year and I think it is to Carol's eternal credit that from the outset, she made it quite clear that I was free to play cricket as often and whenever I pleased. After two or three years my response to this gesture was I believe equally magnanimous, when I confirmed that I would drop out of the annual match on Christmas Morning so that I would not be late for dinner.

Looking at the picture generally, there's little opportunity for chatting up on the club cricket circuit as surprisingly, attractive unescorted ladies can, I gather, find more exciting things to do than watch cricket. Most of the chat therefore, goes on within the club between wives and girl-friends with the odd swop around from time to time, to keep things interesting.

I can only think of the rare occasion when a member of my club successfully managed to chat up a female attached to the opposition, but one that springs to mind occurred at Crowhurst Park one year. Their wicket-keeper, probably in his late forties at the time, had a very comely daughter whom he had trained to great proficiency with regard to teas, etc. In the pub afterwards one of the lads successfully engineered a date and I understand a mini romance blossomed for a few weeks. Naturally, this was the source of much dressing room banter, and pathetic attempts were made to compose a suitable limerick. I think as far as anyone got went something like:

'She was only the wicket-keeper's daughter; but she knew how to whip 'em off.'

A 'chatting up' story I particulary relish occurred on a rugger club tour to Lille in France in my distant bachelor days. The tour was just for a long weekend and the details are now lost in an alcoholic blurr of riotous goings-on in dingy cafes. On the last night our hosts, anxious to please, laid on a formal dinner, followed by a 'disco' for 'le dancing'. Of course, the major problem was to find enough spare women to satisfy thirty half-crazed Englishmen, but in the event they managed to muster a dozen or so girls, mainly daughters of older players, wives or girl-friends let out on a short leash. We tarted ourselves up as best we could, a process I knew to be a waste of time, as I would simply get trampled on in the rush. One chap, a certain David Wilkins, appeared immaculately dressed for the occasion in three-piece suit complete with polka-dot handkerchief and everything greased, creased and gleaming. Behind the stiff upper lip, David had an impish

87

sense of humour and pulled off a masterstroke when 'le dancing' commenced. One of the first away on the signal for the off, he successfully engaged a very tall, willowy, innocent-looking French girl of about seventeen in conversation, although she spoke only a few words of English. They moved sedately round the floor in perfect ballroom dancing position doing a slow foxtrot, irrespective of the music being played, whilst painfully attempting to communicate in a mixture of pigeon French and English. Fascinated by his performance, I watched intently from the side lines, and as he came past me on one circuit, I heard him trying to convey to his partner the fact that the room was getting quite hot and that he might have to take something off.

When this idea was finally transmitted, he excused himself with much bowing and scraping and disappeared for a few seconds into the cloakroom. He returned with no change of expression, having removed his trousers only, while jacket and waistcoat remained firmly buttoned in place. What made his appearance more comical were his knee length long-johns and black socks held neatly in position by suspenders.

As you can imagine, the expression on the girl's face was a mixture of fright, astonishment, embarrassment and just about every other emotion, and I thought for a moment that she would run out of the room screaming hysterically. David's charming smile, however, allayed her fears, and they continued their dance while he conveyed to her how much cooler and more comfortable he felt.

Turning to my cricket colleagues, in this permissive society so many wives or girl-friends have come and gone, that it is increasingly difficult to remember 'who is with whom'. We had a chap who played a few games for us having been strongly recommended by a rival club (not a good omen) and he turned out to be really bad news, cricket-wise. Nevertheless, I felt the selectors were a trifle shortsighted when they dropped him for this reason, as he used to turn up in a Rolls-Bentley accompanied by a dishy, elegant blonde dressed as if going to a Palace garden party.

They never used to have tea with the proletariat, as she would produce a hamper from the back of the Rolls with collapsible table, silver teapot, etc. and they would then picnic on their own. I imagine we would have been quite incapable of chatting her up, but we might have achieved the worthwhile secondary objective of securing an invitation to tea.

Another chap who played a few games for us in the late sixties was a test pilot, Charles, a very useful cricketer, but he was always winging off to Bogata or jetting back from Caracas, minutes before the beginning, or at the end, of a match. He had the complete jet-set image with E-type sports car, flat in town, and a succession of frothy birds who never seemed to know what side of the date line they were on. I was Captain of the side for one match at Preston Park and Charles made his usual late entry with a young lady in tow wearing a full-length silver lame dress and looking somewhat dishevelled, presumably from the night before. As often happens, we had no scorer so while I was wondering what to do about this, Charles volunteered that Veronica would be only too happy to perform. Naturally, I jumped at the offer and only found out later that she'd never scored before, on a cricket ground anyway, but she did her best and the two scorers agreed totals at the end of the day, give or take a few runs.

In the pub afterwards, I did the usual chores of buying everyone drinks and collecting match fees, and then felt constrained to thank Veronica for her assistance in our hour of need. As she clearly operated on a higher social plane, I approached her rather timidly and said something like:

'Thank you very much for scoring, Veronica. Can I fetch you a half'? She looked at me suspiciously and then gave the cool measured reply, 'If you mean would I like a drink, thank you. I'll have a pernod, grenadine, ice and water.'

Concentrating heavily on this complex list, I ordered up, and was shattered to be charged five shillings and fourpence which in those days was the equivalent of two and a half pints of best bitter. Clutching the glass carefully with both hands. I passed it to her, and then 'retired hurt', making a mental note to charge it up to expenses.

Carol and I have been married for some years now and, struggling under the burden of mortgage, rates, insurance, etc., my pips are squeaking as loudly as the next man's. On top of the financial there's the baby-sitting problem but, nevertheless, I feel morally obliged to take Carol out every three months or so, if only to see the light of day.

We live on a new estate and the current form of entertainment is the disco party, so when we received an invitation recently I agreed to come home straight after the match in order to put in an appearance. Our neighbour stated that the occasion was an

89

informal one and that we were to 'come as we were' and to 'make ourselves at home'. Carol immediately booked up permanent residence at the hairdresser's and put the family on starvation diet in order to finance a new dress. When the great day arrived I made a determined effort to tidy myself up with full ablutions including a bottle of deodorant which must of course be 'splashed on all over'.

So far I had earned full marks from my spouse for effort and performance and even scored bonus points by remembering to enthuse ecstatically about her stunning appearance. Unhappily I went straight into the dog-house after our first dance, as she reckoned I had taken our host's invitation too literally. I don't know what all the heat and aggravation was about as, after all, she had given them to me for a recent birthday present.

Apparently the cause of the fuss was simply that I had worn my new carpet slippers.

12. On Tour

Until 1973, St. James's had never had a regular annual tour, and my experiences, therefore, in this department are somewhat limited. To be quite honest, I have heard so many stories, about golf before breakfast, an all day match, booze in the bar all evening, and then an all night card session, that I've always felt I haven't got the physical strength and stamina to last the pace for more than a couple of days. One Bachanalian orgy is enough for me to require a week's recuperation, rather than the other way round.

I did, in fact, go on part of the Preston Nomads tour to the Isle of Wight around 1963 and this experience, whilst most enjoyable, did help me to pin-point a fundamental problem with all club cricket tours. If the men go away on their own for a week, then the wives complain about being left, while their husbands make hay or perhaps make it 'in the hay'. This complaint can be further aggravated by the husband later admitting that he has spent all his cash and can't take the family on their annual holiday that year. On the other hand, if wives accompany the menfolk, they tend to complain about being left to mooch around all day during the match, while the husbands are not too happy about the fact that their activities in certain directions are severely restricted.

Mention of the Nomads Tour gives me the opportunity to say a few words about Trevor Adcock who, by general consent, is the finest club cricketer to have played regularly in Sussex since the war. Perhaps Trevor would consider that he was at the height of his powers in the early sixties. He has scored more than eighty centuries and is still going strong for Steyning and Henfield. A left-handed batsman, he strikes the ball with frightening power and was a decidedly swift bowler until a knee injury forced him to become an above average leg-spinner. To complete the Sobers image, he was also a brilliant cover field.

Trevor used to take part regularly in the Nomads Tour to the I.o.W. and when he was unable to go in 1963, the local paper stated with an almost audible sigh of relief that the Nomads were without: 'The Bradman of amateur cricket in Sussex'. I detail below a few simple facts about his tour performances, which are typical of his career as a whole.

In 1959, Trevor scored 227 runs in 5 innings, 3 times not out, including a century against Newport and also took 4 for 20 against Ryde. He returned in 1960, which was a vintage year for him, when he scored 107 and took 5 for 46 against the Police on the Wednesday, scored 160 not out against Newport on the Thursday, and thrashed 97 against Gosport on the Saturday. In a total of 7 innings that year he scored 526 runs, half of which came in sixes and fours with an average of 87·6.

A poor 1961 tour followed, as only three matches were played due to the weather, but nevertheless he took 8 for 41 against Shanklin and then scored 133 not out against Burgess Hill who also happened to be touring the Island. In 1962, he had a fairly quiet time, taking 5 for 45 against Shanklin, scoring 63 against the Police, another 5 wickets for 20 runs against Newport, and then hammered 97 against J.S. Whites XI on the last day.

Unhappily I can't claim to be more than a casual aquaintance, but I'm always interested in anyone in the super-star category. I remember driving into the Steyning ground around two o'clock one Saturday a few years back, and my respect for Trevor doubled instantly when I saw him on his way to the wicket to put the stumps in—a super-star doing the domestic chores is an unusual sight.

As skipper of the team, he was anxious to give his team-mates a fair crack of the whip. Steyning batted after tea and needed about 180 to win. He seemed almost reluctant to come to the wicket, and finally appeared at number seven when things had 'gone a little dark' for his side. He soon got down to business and generally sorted things out with some devastating hitting down to the tennis courts at the bottom end. John Harrison was our bowler, an extremely accurate spinner, but Trevor made it look as if he was being offered half-volleys in some sort of contrived arrangement, so that he could gain a long distance hitting record. He seemed to walk further and further down the track, hitting each ball longer and harder; a fact I ruefully remember as I was fielding at deep mid-off.

In 1973, St. James's C.C. arranged a weekend tour to St. Bees School in Cumberland, as the result of a kind invitation by the headmaster, Geoff Lees, who has lived in Brighton and played for Sussex 2nd XI. On the first tour we played just two all day matches against the School XI on Saturday, and then a select XI raised by David Marshall on the Sunday. David is a House Master at the School and has also lived in Brighton and played for St. James's in the past. Some players travelled up on the Thursday to get in some golf, and the rest on the Friday, and in a modest way, I established something of a record for my performances on this tour. As twelve of us had set off, we drew straws to decide who should drop out of the Saturday match and naturally I was the unlucky individual. On the Saturday night we were treated to a magnificent banquet by the School cook, and as we circulated like vultures around a large table laden with everything from prawn cocktail to partridge curry, our glasses were charged by an enthusiastic team of prefects. My team-mates claim that when I woke up on the Sunday morning with an agonising stomach-ache, it was due to excessive eating, though I'm confident that the cause of the malaise was a grumbling appendix. In any event I was too ill to perform, so I returned home on the Monday having travelled nearly eight hundred miles and not having picked up a ball in anger.

St. Bees School must be the ideal place to be educated. A few hundred yards from the sea, it dominates a small town and has just about every conceivable amenity, as well as maintaining a first class educational standard. A promising all round games player, would I think, be worn out by the end of the term as he can do his thing on the cricket ground, rugger pitch, tennis court, swimming pool, squash or five courts and athletics track. If that isn't enough, he could then go for a round on the School golf course.

Incredible to relate, the Headmaster invited us again in 1974 and we arranged a game on the preceding Friday which unfortunately was rained off. In spite of some unseemly behaviour in the local hostelry, we managed to keep the slate reasonably clean, and went back again in 1975, with an afternoon match on the Friday against Cockermouth, in addition to the usual Saturday and Sunday fixtures. David Marshall had also arranged that on the Thursday evening we would play a limited over match against Eskdale, as a suitable way to start the tour. The more I think about that Thursday evening and reflect back over my cricket career, the more convinced I am that Eskdale is the perfect

By Courtesy: Henfield C.C.

Trevor Adcock of Steyning and Henfield C.C.s

Genuine 'Super Star'—yet ready to do the chores

example of the rustic cricket ground. Everything seemed to fit one's image of country village cricket at the turn of the century and I apologise in advance if I wax eloquent for a few paragraphs.

Most of the team had travelled to Cumberland on the Wednesday, but Charles Harrison, Roger Green and myself set off from Sussex around nine o'clock Thursday morning with our instructions: 'Eskdale, near the Bower House, six o'clock start'. It's a fairly comfortable journey on the motorways and when we drove into Eskdale on a fine spring evening it was only five o'clock. Cruising through the village, we kept our eyes open for a cricket ground but were soon through to the other side, so we turned back and went along a couple of other roads before we finally spotted the Bower House. It was an appetising looking pub, with the car-park behind and, pulling up, we staggered out to stretch our legs, taking a quick look at some cows grazing in the field behind, before strolling off to try to find the ground. After we had quizzed several locals, we arrived back in the car-park to take a closer look at the field behind. Leaning on the fence 'cowpoke style' we spotted the pitch and pavilion in a field adjacent to the one at the back of the park.

94

It was a magnificent sight. Just one chap (obviously a domestic) half-changed, pushed a hand mower down the pitch, his wife busying herself with whitewash and brushes while in the background stood a tiny wooden pavilion screened by trees. Anxious to see more, we entered the first field, gingerly negotiating the cow-dung, before passing through a gate into the second, where the under-foot hazard switched to sheep's turds. Sheep were, in fact, grazing around and on the pitch, with the grass progressively shorter towards the centre. Having greeted the chap busily mowing, we were politely speechless, as we watched the mower bounce between bumps on the wicket.

The pavilion also caught the eye, a superb example of antique rudimentary woodwork, no more than 20ft wide by 10ft. Treading the steps, pitted with stud marks, we entered a dank, musty museum of village cricket. In one corner was the changing room, an area about 6ft by 8ft, with no door, inside which were a few old chairs, some rusty nails on the walls, and two old mirrors cracked and long since fallen from eye level. Another corner housed the groundsman's equipment, while an ancient perished leather cricket bag lurked behind the door. We also noticed a special metal dust-pan for removing turds, soon busily employed and I was particularly struck by various articles of cricket apparel, perched on a ledge: one glove, a decaying yellow pad and three old balls each vomiting string down to the floor.

Our sentimental journey was ended by players arriving and we got on with a twenty-over match around 6.30. The game also marked a personal milestone, as I bowled my longest-ever spell of slow off-spin in club cricket. Brought on at the bottom end to contain the hard hitting opposition, I managed to impart such vicious spin to the ball that my second delivery passed clean over the batsman's head! From 6 successive overs I returned the excellent figures of 1 for 46, and we won a marvellous match by 10 runs. With a convivial evening in the Bower House afterwards it was an ideal start to the tour which had three further games and finished on the Sunday evening.

The session after the Sunday match became delightfully uninhibited and I have never ceased to marvel at the lyricism and inventiveness of the songs as we went on into the small hours. With unlimited kitty the beer flowed like water until some over enthusiastic soul insisted on buying a round of Port rapidly followed by another of Campari. This tended to confuse the

Eskdale C.C., Cumbria

This panoramic view shows the Ground Staff hard at work

palate and certain members were forced to leave the scene somewhat rapidly, foregoing the usual courtesies.

What possesses a mature, middle-aged chap to dance down
St. Bees High Street at five o'clock in the morning, arm in arm
with a colleague waving an empty wine bottle, while singing a
'Sea Shanty'?

Some of the all-time greats such as Hobbs, Bradman, Hutton
and Sobers were awarded knighthoods, and lesser decorations
have been handed out to many other top performers. As far as I
know, these awards have never extended down to the game at
club cricket level but if they were, then something equivalent to a
Distinguished Service Medal should be given to Robin Forbes
and his two colleagues who made up the Mayfield C.C. Touring
Team to Surrey in 1955.

Mayfield C.C. are a fine old mid-Sussex club formally established
in 1866 but, like everyone else, have their ups and downs with
regard to playing strength and, in this instance, availability.

Robin Forbes was captain of the club from 1955 to 1960, a wicket keeper/batsman of star quality but above all, a dedicated and fanatically keen club cricketer. He had many contacts in London and the South-East and at the beginning of the 1955 season he thought it would be a good idea to arrange a week's tour and play sides in the Surrey area. Although Surrey and Sussex are adjacent counties, twenty years ago car ownership was still the exception rather than the rule, and thus a thirty mile journey was quite a trip.

As often happens, after much initial enthusiasm from his team-mates, as the departure date drew near, all sorts of reasons cropped up to prevent people from going on the tour. Mayfield had their normal Saturday and Sunday fixtures on the preceding week-end and the arrangements were that the tour party would move up to a hotel near Caterham on the Sunday evening and then move around from there to play the fixtures. Rumour has it that Robin Forbes, who drove a large Land-Rover at the time, fitted a trawl net which could be flung out from the back to scoop up any unsuspecting passers-by!

When the deadline arrived on Sunday evening the basic tour party consisted of Robin Forbes, his wife Elspeth, and two other players, John Whipp and Peter Freeman. Fortunately Elspeth, skilled at umpiring, scoring and tea-making, was also adept at charming the opposition players into making up the numbers. John Whipp was a useful batsman, but Peter Freeman was a self-confessed domestic, happy to fill-in and do all the odd chores. As the saying goes, 'some are born stars and some have stardom thrust upon them', and in Peter Freeman's case this materialised in the shape of a red leather ball. He was asked to project this object for two or three hours a day during the tour, as near as he could to the opposing batsmen.

Forbes, although a little disappointed at the strength and depth of his side, was not too concerned about the first match at Ightam near Sevenoaks as eight other Mayfield players agreed to travel up for the day which happened to be a Bank Holiday. It was a routine game which they won fairly comfortably and later that evening Forbes bade what must have been a tearful farewell to the eight from Mayfield, who returned home ready for work on Tuesday.

During the evening session though, he plied the opposition with ale and enlisted their sympathy so that three of them agreed to turn out for the next match at Whyteleafe. This gave him a theoretical six for the match, although word of his plight was spreading fast by jungle telegraph. When the Mayfield three arrived at Whyteleafe on Tuesday morning only two Ightam players were there, and although everyone scoured the shrubbery and the pavilion loft, when Forbes went out to toss up with the opposing skipper, he had only five men on the ground.

In retrospect, Robin Forbes believes that this moment was the highlight of the tour. The skippers went through the ritual of examining the track, fixing the intervals, and rejoicing that the weather was just right for a game of cricket. Finally the agonising moment came and the coin went up, but Forbes gasped a sigh of relief when he called correctly and without a moment's hesitation invited Whyteleafe to bat. At this point the conversation went something like this:

'Actually, Skipper, I'm afraid we're a little short at the moment.'

'Oh dear, that's unfortunate. Can I offer you a sub?'

'Well, actually, there's one chap who should be here shortly, but er . . . basically we're six short.'

'Six short ! ! ! ! !'

'Yes, we ummm . . . we've had one or two problems ! ! !'

'Good grief, old man, are you serious?'

Fortunately, the Whyteleafe skipper had a sense of humour and after further explanation Mayfield took the field with six men including one sub. Forbes watched the entrance to the ground anxiously in case anything looking remotely like a cricketer should appear, and about midday two players turned up more or less out of the blue.

Mayfield, therefore, settled down with seven as their final total and they managed to get Whyteleafe all out for 140. In reply, Forbes opened the batting effectively, on 0 for 4, but he got his head down and the game developed into a real cliff-hanger with Mayfield scrambling home at 141 for 5, their last pair at the wicket and Forbes 80 not out.

Elated by this success, Forbes won the sympathy of the Whyteleafe players so that five promised to turn out for the Wednesday match against Caterham. In addition, by continuous use of the index finger they managed to raise three other players from various parts of the South of England so that, with his basic tour party, he had a theoretical eleven for the next game and no doubt slept soundly that night.

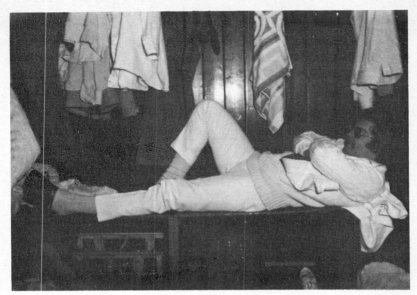

Next man in!

The Mayfield team set off for the Caterham ground on the Wednesday morning with the arrangement that they would meet four of the Whyteleafe players in a pub on the way. Although they waited until the last possible moment they did not show, so at the ground their eleven had been reduced to seven. Disappointed, Forbes once again scoured the shrubbery and in fact found two spare Caterham players to give him a satisfactory nine at the start of the game. On this occasion he lost the toss, was put in to bat and Mayfield were shot out for seventy but a strange thing happened in the Caterham innings. Inexplicably Peter Freeman made the ball swing violently and he took 5 for 30 before the opposition scraped home by 3 wickets.

In the bar after the match, Forbes had a far more difficult task, because the Thursday game was against the Old Elizabethans at Barnet in North London, and he was unable to cajole any of the Caterham players into helping him out. They were, however, very interested in the Friday fixture against Warlingham— something of a local needle match—so he readily enlisted the help of three quick bowlers eager to settle some old scores. Demoralised, Forbes, his wife and two colleagues called on their vast resources of stamina and small change, and phoned around to get promises from four players from the Sidcup area and two from Finchley, to give them nine for the Thursday game, which at that stage of the Tour was quite acceptable.

When Mayfield arrived at Barnet on Thursday, Forbes counted heads and two of his fill-ins had failed to show, so he had seven, but the Old Elizabethans offered one spare and he was able to start the match with eight. Unhappily, this time they could not put up much of a performance and, batting first, were all out for around 100 and lost by 10 wickets. Closeted in the bar afterwards, Forbes had little chance of getting his opponents to travel to Warlingham for the Friday match. He had the three Caterham players, however, so he decided to issue a cry from the wilderness and phoned around the Mayfield players back home with his tale of woe, and managed to persuade two to travel up. He gave up any further efforts for players, therefore, with a theoretical eight.

When he arrived at Warlingham on Friday morning and went through the dreaded head counting routine, he must have been on his knees. If he had put his hands together for help from the heavens, the response was quick and crystal clear in the form of large and numerous drops of rain. When the opposition skipper suggested at lunch that the game would have to be called off, Forbes tried hard to conceal his enthusiastic agreement.

The Touring Team arrived home on Friday evening, shattered but proud of their epic achievement.

After he had completed the weekend fixtures, Robin Forbes had a week off, but for the next fortnight was involved every day in the Mayfield Festival, and he worked out afterwards that he had played twenty-three games within twenty-nine consecutive days. I hope that by recounting fairly full details of the amazing feat of Robin Forbes and his three man tour, any team secretary cursing his luck at being one short on a Saturday morning, will consider himself relatively well off and just keep on dialling.

13. Stories

The fund of cricket club stories is limitless, and I have not attempted to fill up this book by scouring the earth for new material. Nevertheless, over the last couple of years I've made a point of asking cricketers I've played with, or against, what they think is the funniest thing they've seen on a cricket field. The replies given are interesting in that in many cases people recall a specific incident which needs detailed character sketches of the people involved, plus masses of relevant background information in order to appear humorous to an outsider. Thinking further on this, within a particular team, much of the humour generated is by 'geeing up' and 'mickey taking' which, to be understood by anyone else, requires knowledge that 'Arthur' wears blue polka-dot underpants, or that 'Fred' is a left-handed glass blower. The few stories I have jotted down in this chapter are an entirely personal selection, tickling my warped sense of humour and hopefully not necessitating long-winded explanation to appeal to a wider audience.

My old colleague, Derek Pickering, relates a story of a match held during the Brighton College Cricket Week one year, between Old Brightonians and Incogniti. On the morning of the match the opposition indicated apologetically that they were one short and wondered whether the Old Boys could find someone to make up the side. There was no-one available at the eleventh hour except a young Frenchman, who had turned up at the ground to watch his first game of cricket and further his education into our peculiar habits. Unable to speak more than a few words of English, Pierre was a prime target and was duly pounced on, press-ganged into performing, and kitted out, probably before he realised what was going on.

Incogniti fielded first, and Pierre was stationed harmlessly enough at mid-off, where he stood watching the spectacle with an air of bemused interest. For twenty minutes or so he was not called upon to do anything, until an off drive was pushed fairly gently towards him. Having watched the progress of the ball carefully, Pierre waited until the last moment before falling onto it rugger style but, timing his dive too late, he missed and the ball ran on out to deep mid-off. Undaunted, he sprang to his feet and chased after it enthusiastically, then dived on it again when it had more or less stopped. Grabbing hold of the ball he jumped to his feet and held it aloft, with a beam of triumph spreading across his face. By now the batsman had completed three, and set off for a fourth, as Pierre made no attempt to throw the ball in. While he remained like the Statue of Liberty, the other fielders started shouting instructions in a rising crescendo, as the batsmen scampered up and down the track like two-year-olds. Although he couldn't understand what was being said, he finally got the drift that something was awry by the frantic gesticulations being produced. He decided that extra cover was making the most noise, so hurled the ball desperately in that direction. Amazed, extra cover could do little more than duck instinctively, and thereafter everyone subsided into laughter, with the batsmen, of course, laughing loudest of all.

One of the stock situations of club cricket, or of any cricket for that matter, is the disputed l.b.w. or caught behind decision. Watching a batsman storm off the pitch, foaming at the mouth, before perhaps throwing his bat through the pavilion window, is not a common occurrence but it's by no means unique. I remember a fiery young gentleman, having been given out l.b.w. in the first over of the match who threw his bat through the pavilion window then changed and left the ground without saying a word to anyone.

There's also the true story of a very well known star performer in Sussex cricket who must remain nameless, who stormed off the pitch hurling his bat through the pavilion window from some twenty yards out. A colleague, quietly padding up inside, was a fraction irritated by being nearly decapitated, apart from being showered by broken glass. Picking up the offending weapon he hurled it back through another window, whereupon it whistled past the incoming batsman at waist height. I understand the two men then engaged in what is diplomatically called 'a full and frank exchange of views'.

Perhaps the best story I've heard on this theme was told to me by a chap down on holiday from the North, and I didn't get the full facts and details of the match apart from the particular incident. I gather that the batsman involved had been playing

102

for many years and always ground away all afternoon to pile up his runs, and on this occasion was given out, to what he thought was an atrocious l.b.w. decision, when not far short of his fifty. Absolutely furious, he protested strongly to the umpire, before he was eventually persuaded to leave the wicket and appeared to have calmed down as he went into the pavilion. In fact, anger was burning like a furnace inside him, because he got changed, walked out to his van parked by the ground, and drove it straight onto the field. He pulled up right across the middle of the wicket, jammed the brake on, locked the door and stalked off, presumably to catch a bus or walk home.

I don't know what happened next, but the thought does occur to me that they could possibly have got on with the game using only very slow bowlers!

Another situation, ripe for humour, is where the batsmen get mixed up in their calling and end up at the same end, or collide in mid-wicket. Referring again to Derek Pickering, who has been playing for St. James's for twenty years now, he insists that the most remarkable match he's played in for the club was against Rottingdean at Stanmer Park in 1957. Rottingdean batted first and were all out for 19, and St. James's managed to make incredibly hard work of scoring the runs. We did, in fact, slump to 17 for 9 with two semi-retired fill-in players at the wicket. When what turned out to be the last ball was bowled, the striker swung hard and got a top edge to put up a fairly easy catch about halfway down the track. The wicket-keeper, bowler, mid-on and cover point converged to the anticipated landing point, plus the two batsmen who were, of course, anxious to scamper a vital run. As can be imagined, a glorious pile up occurred, with six bodies spread all over the place and ball buried somewhere in the middle. One of the fielders was the first to recover his senses and got up, grabbed the ball, and hurled it at the stumps at the bowler's end. It missed, and thus four overthrows were scored to give St. James's victory by one wicket.

John Maynard is a business colleague of mine and he told me of a glorious running mix-up, during one of those extended lunches one is forced to endure in the line of duty. John was playing for the Mediators, an Essex club, on tour along the Kent and Sussex coast, in a match against Folkestone. He opened the batting with a chap appropriately called Pat Shott, who went off like the proverbial gun from the start and reached his fifty in double quick time, with John playing a domestic rôle. Hitting the ball very hard, Shott eventually seemed to have overdone it by lofting a very high catch straight to long-on.

John cantered down the wicket, glancing over his shoulder and when he reached the other end, saw the catch dropped, but turned to find himself face to face with Pat who had not moved. John immediately set off to regain his ground and, as he neared the other end, was relieved to see a wild throw from the fielder miss the stumps and waiting bowler by yards. As he halted just past the crease, he was surprised to hear heavy breathing and footsteps behind him, and he turned to find himself again face to face with the other batsman. Again he set off for the other end, and as he ran he watched third man field the ball and hurl it in to the wicket-keeper's end. Fortunately, it was another wild throw, forcing the keeper to dive full-length, and palm the ball towards a non-existent square-leg. John cantered home, but again heard even heavier breathing and footsteps behind him and turned to find himself yet again face to face with Pat Shott. This time, exasperated, he grabbed him by the shoulders, pointing to the other end said, 'Look, you stay here, and I'll go down there'. John set off and just made his ground, thereby completing four with his colleague having run two, and neither batsman having crossed at any point between the batting creases.

There are many stories of the apocryphal or after-dinner type and I would like to include just one told me by Tony Sweetman concerning a match in the West Indies, which I understand was originally related in this country by a chap called Constantine! ! The story concerns the last over in an important league match watched by a sizeable and partisan crowd, restless and vociferous after a long hot day in the sun.

At the start of the last over the situation was that the last pair of the home team were at the wicket needing eight runs to win, with their umpire at the bowler's end. After the striker had swung and missed at the first two balls, the bowler's umpire decided on some positive assistance to his team. To the third ball he called 'No ball' well before it was delivered with the bowler, indeed, not even in his delivery stride. This time, fortunately, the batsman swung successfully and dispatched it over the mid-wicket, first bounce for four. With four balls left and four required, the striker again swung unsuccessfully at the next three deliveries so that four runs were required off the last ball. With the tension unbearable, again the bowler's umpire got into the act calling 'No ball', but unhappily the batsman failed to connect, so that with one ball left, three runs were still required. Feeling that he'd done enough to assist his team, the home umpire allowed the ball to be bowled and to frenzied cheers from the crowd the striker connected fairly firmly and the batsmen scampered up and down the wicket, as long-on raced in to field. Having completed two, they went for an impossible third run, and a fine throw from the fielder shattered the stumps, with the batsman still yards from his ground. As the visiting side unleashed a chorus of appeals, along with victory dance, the home umpire called a clear 'Not out', to clinch the game for his side.

Watching all this helplessly from square-leg, the visiting umpire, desperate to do his bit, seized on his one and only chance. Turning towards the scorers, he touched both shoulders at once and bellowed out, 'Two short'. I trust the poor fellow was lynched by the home crowd in a decent and humane manner.

A true story of a remarkable finish was in the match between Linden Park and Haywards Heath 2nd XI's five years ago. The home side, Haywards Heath, were in the field and, with one ball remaining, Linden Park required four runs to win with their last pair at the wicket. After much preparation by all concerned, the ball was eventually delivered to which the batsman projected a frantic swipe but only managed to get a thick edge and send the ball in a gentle arc towards mid-wicket. The simple catch was dropped and the fielder, absolutely furious with himself, picked up the ball and hurled it towards the stumps. From close range he missed by yards, and it carried on to the boundary for four over-throws. In the space of two seconds, therefore, victory for the home side had been turned into defeat, but retribution for the offender was both swift and painful. A spectator, incensed at this outrage, fielded the ball as it crossed the boundary and flung it powerfully back towards the wicket where it struck the player smack in the back of the neck! !

I believe elsewhere in this book I've described Ian Boyd-Pain as one of the finest bull-shitters around, but his tale of an incident in a match between Brighton Nomads and the Army Intelligence Corps at Maresfield seemed too incredible to be true. To verify the story, therefore, I collared B.P. in the bar one evening, pinned

The great B.-P. inculcating the mythology of spin bowling to the younger generation

him to the wall by his lapels and brought my knee up into a sensitive area. Asking him to repeat his story from that position, he managed to do so with not too many variations from the original so I'll proceed as follows:

The Nomads team arrived at the camp gatehouse in three cars and, as they pulled up at the guard-house, were challenged by a zealous young N.C.O. with cap peak glued to his nose, to provide name, permit, password, etc. Taken aback there was silence for a few seconds before some-one in the first car volunteered casually, 'Good grief old chap, we're only here to play cricket'. To which the N.C.O.'s immediate reply was, 'Oh sorry, Sir, the pitch is straight on down the road to the right'.

When they found the pitch it turned out to be of rudimentary nature, best described as an area of grassland given a 'short back 'n sides' by a disgruntled Private on 'fatigues'.

Anyway, they got changed and the match got under way with the Army side fielding first, and led by a Major Smithers who looked suitably intelligent and studious, and also obviously came from the right school. The rest of the Army side looked distinctly domestic in appearance, probably Other Ranks ordered to volunteer for the game.

The first incident took place when the Major came on to bowl some highly theoretical leg breaks, while the Other Ranks dozed quietly in the outfield. Requiring an alteration to his field at the end of an over he called out to long-on, but was unable to attract his attention. Slipping back on to the parade ground he finally bellowed out, 'Johnson!' Reacting as if shot, Johnson sprang to attention and saluted, shouting, 'S——i——r', in reply. With everyone highly amused, the Major had the last word when he called back, 'Not without your cap on, man.'

Having made a reasonable score by five o'clock the Nomads declared and everyone trooped off to a Nissen hut for tea. The hut was sparsely furnished with wooden tables and benches and the Nomads were surprised to find only two or three plates piled high with slices of bread, covered in a substance looking suspiciously like margarine. After a couple of minutes a Private came round and dished out huge mugs of sweet tea, then after a further break, one of the Nomads voiced the thoughts and fears of many with a hoarse whisper, 'Where's the bleedin' cakes then?'

However the Army had bigger ideas, and eventually a Corporal came round and plonked a huge plateful of fish and chips in front of each surprised player. It may, of course, have been a simple ploy to immobilize them in the field.

The match continued with the Army batting and after an hour or so an astonishing and macabre incident occurred. The Nomads bowler who was reasonably quick, pitched a shorter ball, and the batsman going for the hook, missed and was struck a nasty blow on the side of the temple. He slumped backwards across the stumps, while the ball was deflected down to fine leg. The non-striker, watching the ball, called for a run and got down to the other end before he realized that his partner was in no way responding. Sensing the danger of being run out, he turned and ran back down the track to regain his ground as fine-leg threw a flat fast return to the bowler's wicket. When the non-striker was two or three yards from home he was hit smack on the back of the head, causing him to dive inert across the stumps.

The situation had thus arrived that both batsmen were lying unconscious on the ground with the woodwork entirely demolished and all available first aid resources were urgently summoned onto the field. One batsman was carried off and had to have hospital treatment, while the other was revived sufficiently to be helped back to the pavilion.

In previous years the Nomads had been invited into the Sergeants' Mess for a few pints with the opposition after the match. On this occasion, by way of a special honour, Major Smithers invited them to join him in the Officers' Mess. With the invitation gratefully accepted there was only one snag to the arrangement. As he was the only officer playing, the Nomads said goodbye to the rest of the Army team and went inside to drink with, and chat to, the Major!

Man's inhumanity to man is not a subject one likes to associate with club cricket, but it features strongly in Peter Beecheno's story concerning our old friend, Noel Bennett.

Noel was tossing up his ultra-slows from the bottom end one day when the batsman selected a particular delivery and hammered it vertically upwards with ferocious power. Ever the optimist, Noel shouted a confident 'Mine!!' and started to shuffle about in the projected landing area. Unhappily, in doing so he tripped himself up and fell to his knees losing his spectacles in the process. As he scrambled about on all fours trying to find them, the ball still swirling around in the upper atmosphere overhead, several of his colleagues decided to come to the rescue. They ran in from various directions to attempt the catch but were stopped dead in their tracks by a stern command from square leg:

'Leave it!! He called for it—let's see if it hits 'im!'

Fortunately, the ball plummeted to earth, missing Noel's head by a few feet, and he remains with us, therefore, in both flesh and spirit.

My last and favourite story which plumbs the depths of misfortune on a cricket field, will appeal only to those with a really sick sense of humour. Details of the incident, which took place in a match between Reading and Teddington in 1957, were passed to me by Peter Withers who recently joined our club. Both sides contained good club cricketers and Peter Withers was bowling medium-pace, to a batsman a bit past his prime who'd been in a for a few overs. The circumstances of the batsman's demise are almost too painful to relate.

Peter bowled a shortish delivery and the batsman went for the hook, but as often happens, only managed to get a thick top edge. The ball ricocheted on to his cheekbone, before lobbing into the waiting hands of second slip. As he finished the shot, legs straddled across the wicket, he fell under the force of the blow, thereby impaling himself painfully on the off-stump. Simultaneously, gasping with the shock, his false teeth popped out to land somewhere around the crease. Peter Withers, following through and alarmed by the havoc he had initiated, rushed down the wicket to attend to the batsman, but in doing so trod on and smashed his false teeth. The incredible picture thus forms in my mind of the poor unfortunate fellow limping painfully towards the pavilion, bat under arm, broken false teeth in one hand, with the other hand attempting to staunch the flow of blood from his cheek! !

14. A Rose among Thorns

For years now, I've had sculling around in my memory the picture of just one ball in a match which I stumbled upon quite by chance. It made such an impression on me that I must attempt to commit the details to paper by way of explanation.

By process of elimination, I think the year must have been 1964, and during that summer I was staying in digs at Woking in Surrey. Fortunately, this arrangement did not affect my weekend cricket for St. James's as I travelled over there on a Monday morning and came back on Friday evening. As I didn't know anyone locally, I was generally at a loose end in the evenings, although I was supposed to be studying for examinations. I found my digs, really just a single room, claustrophobic in the warmer weather so I used to set off on various walks around the area, which generally tended to end up in the pub at the corner of the road.

The particular evening was right at the height of the summer, and I can only resort to the corny description of calling it 'balmy'. I set off at a leisurely pace from my digs, deciding to aim for the local park, if only to work up a thirst before diving into the local. I wouldn't know where the park is now, but it was quite extensive, with clumps of bushes and the odd tree every now and then and endless asphalt paths leading in all directions. Choosing one at random I strolled along, tactfully averting my eyes from the various courting couples spread-eagled in the shrubbery.

Having travelled perhaps a couple of hundred yards, I'd just about decided that I had gone far enough when I turned a corner, and happened upon what I eventually worked out to be a cricket match. I choose those words carefully, because I certainly didn't immediately recognise the fact as the usual guide lines such as pitch, boundary, pavilion, etc., all appeared to be missing. Apart from that, at the point I arrived on the scene, there seemed to be nothing happening. Stopping dead in my tracks, I gazed in astonishment at the performers, who stood like statues at random intervals, over an area about fifty yards. In the centre of the clearing were two sets of stumps and I eventually worked out that the game was held up pending the arrival of a new batsman.

Recovering from my shock, I took a closer look round and counted fifteen fielders with some half-dozen other bodies sprawled among various items of discarded apparel about forty yards from the stumps. These, presumably, were the batting side but there was no score board, nor any other clues to connect the occasion with a cricket match.

As I looked around at the players, I can only describe them as a motley looking crew, mostly in their late teens, with the longer hair-style, which was coming into fashion at that time. No one on the pitch wore anything resembling cricket kit, although two or three of them wore white plimsolls with, at the best, light grey flannels. The chap standing nearest to me, in a position vaguely deep mid-wicket, hit me right between the eyes. He was wearing a smart red track-suit, with his footwear a pair of perfectly bulled up army boots. Woking, of course, is not far from Pirbright and Aldershot, and he stood there as if on the parade ground at the 'at ease' position.

Normally when a batsman does not appear reasonably quickly there are signs of irritation from the fielders, with the odd shout of 'Two minutes!'.

I managed to work out, however, that the reason for the delay, being so readily accepted, was that there were only two pairs of pads so that the outgoing batsman had to be stripped before the ingoing could make his entrance.

Having sorted out what was going on, I was highly curious to see the next piece of action. At long last, the new batsman got to his feet, and set off for the wicket, wearing white tennis shirt above light blue gaberdines, with his footwear a lethal looking pair of brown 'winkle-pickers!' The over-employed pads were a forlorn sight, with horse-hair sprouting out at various points and so limp with use that the tops flapped up and down as he walked. His bat was a mahogany brown creation, held together by string and vellum, which had clearly seen better days before he was born.

He approached the crease in traditional callow youth style, bat slung across shoulder, while he slouched along examining his toe-caps. After what seemed an age he got to the wicket and without asking for a guard, just patted his bat down carefully in the existing mark which was presumably in roughly the right position. After a quick almost furtive look round the field, he faced up to his first delivery from a bowler who ran in, off about five yards, and produced quite a reasonable action. There was

111

nothing particularly special about the ball, just a friendly, fairly straight half-volley.

At this point, words begin to fail me, as I've struggled for some time now to try to find a way of describing the stroke he produced. No doubt a trained wordsmith could reel off a perfect description in seconds, but being very much the amateur in that department, I'll have to proceed by a process of elimination. It wasn't in fact a cow, heave or ya-hoo, as those terms would elevate it to a class well above its true status. If you've ever seen an athletics match, or the Olympic Games on television, you will no doubt have observed twenty-five stone giants throwing the hammer vast distances. They swing the thing around their head a few times, then twist round in a circle, and release it by dragging their shoulders out in front of their arms, finishing with a terrifying gasp of breath.

This particular shot, was similar to the last part of a hammer throw, with the batsman seeming to fling his head and shoulders round to leg in agony. Without backlift, he snatched at the bat as if it were fixed to the ground, then wrenched it across, emitting a grunt, while his face was contorted with the effort. At this point he ran into trouble with Newtons Third Law which requires that to every action, there must be an equal and opposite reaction. This violent torque had to be transmitted through the smooth leather soles of his 'pickers to the ground. It was too much to ask, so he spun like a top before ending up on all fours, head towards the stumps.

Had he released the bat, it would certainly have cleared the non-existent boundary, probably decapitating a couple of fielders on the way. In fact, he managed to hang on to it and, incredible to relate, connected with the ball perfectly and sent it screaming off, about a foot above the ground, towards wide mid-on.

My next, and equally difficult, task is to detail what followed. The fielders were as static as they had been while they awaited the new batsman's arrival, although as some concession to action, my soldier friend on the boundary had moved from the 'at ease' position to 'attention'. With little sign of any other movement, however, I fully expected the ball to hurtle unhindered to the boundary and way beyond. To say that mid-on, who had been standing hands behind back, flat-footed and impassive, had other ideas, would be to credit him with mental activity which could not possibly have taken place in the time available. If you imagine a cable attached to his right hand, suddenly jerked sideways with explosive force, this would have the effect of flinging him to the ground like a rag doll. It seemed to happen like that and as he hurtled through the air, arm outstretched, the ball hit the middle of his palm about six inches above the ground. The bullet-like momentum, coupled with the pain of contact, obviously closed his fingers around it, and it stuck there while he completed several somersaults. It was quite definitely the finest catch I've ever seen in any game of cricket and it caused my already sagging jaw to drop lower, as I stood there in disbelief.

In a test match the fielders would have rushed up to congratulate him, and carried him shoulder high round the ground for a lap of honour, to the ecstatic acclaim of the crowd. The level of this game, however, was such that no-one was able to appreciate the fact, and most remained indifferent while two or three applauded politely, or called out 'Well caught, Fred' or whatever.

The batsman clambered to his feet, then slouched off sorrowfully towards the boundary trailing his bat behind him, whilst emitting a stream of highly audible oaths to all and sundry.

As I was in my early twenties at the time, I still had a streak of idealism left and felt, of course, that my cricket was of a considerably superior standard to that which I had just witnessed. My surprise and shock, therefore, turned to indignation, and realising that I would have to wait another three or four minutes to see the next piece of action, I stalked off to continue my walk. In retrospect, that must have been one of the most supercilious and shortsighted things I've done, as who knows what incredible feats may have followed? On the other hand, had I stayed, the memory of that incident would perhaps have been blurred by more mundane events; something I would not like to have happened.

15. The Clouds are High

Having reached the last chapter in my book, I feel that if I have any readers left they must be family or close friends. Consequently, I've allowed myself the luxury of slipping into a reminiscing beard-mumbling frame of mind to consider my cricketing career both past and future.

Trying to fathom out my attachment to cricket and what, if anything, distinguishes the game from many others involving kicking, hitting or bouncing a ball of some sort, much tortuous thought has produced little in the way of closely reasoned argument. Nevertheless, I can perhaps demonstrate the uniqueness of the game by detailing one unimportant incident from a match at Stanmer Park a few years back. It was not particularly funny and, indeed, passed by unheeded by most people present, yet somehow it illustrated the contrasts that can occur if one really looks for them.

We were in the field after tea and to all intents and purposes the match was dead, as with half-an-hour to go the opposition still needed 100 runs to win and we had only taken a few wickets. It was a quiet autumn evening after a cool day, and with no spectators the game had been at stalemate for some time. With everyone acutely aware of the futile charade they were enacting, fielders appeared statuesque and indifferent to the efforts of batsmen and bowler alike, with thoughts on anything but the game in hand.

The batsman at the striker's end looked fairly competent, but had been tied down by accurate bowling and had almost, but not quite, given up any attempt to keep the game alive. Yet again the batsman pushed forward half-heartedly, sending the ball a few yards down the wicket on the off-side and as no-one in the field showed any inclination to retrieve he flirted with the possibility of a quick run. He did, in fact, dart a few yards down the track, but having done so realized that his partner was not only disinterested but unaware of the possibility, as he was leaning on his bat deep in conversation with the umpire.

114

The other optimist on the field was our wicket-keeper who, galvanised into activity, nipped round from behind the stumps to grab the ball, spectacular run-out in mind. As he reached the ball the batsman in the act of turning to regain his ground slipped on to his knees, and our 'keeper, anxious to get back to the stumps by the shortest route, decided to leapfrog over him. Unhappily, as he clambered over the batsman's shoulders, the latter got to his feet and therefore lifted him pick-a-back style. Struggling with this unsolicited load on his shoulders, the batsman staggered a couple of paces until the whole edifice toppled slowly forwards. The two men ended up full length, the 'keeper's arm stretched out about six inches short of the stumps, with the batsman in similar posture, a fraction short of the crease. Exhausted by this burst of activity the two men lay there for a few seconds before scrambling to their feet to recover poise and dignity.

While this mini-drama unfolded, everyone else had remained stock-still and only academically interested, although second slip was sufficiently enthused to offer a desultory 'bad luck 'keeper'. In this instance my emotions were torn three ways: there was the inclination to smirk at the futility of the participants' efforts, concern for their physical well-being and the need to enthuse at our player's run-out attempt. But apart from this personal conflict, we had witnessed hope and optimism, brutally shattered by practical reality, then turned to farce, all in the space of a few seconds. I feel this range and complexity of emotions is somehow peculiar to the fabulous game of cricket.

If you ask any club cricketer what game or games he remembers most vividly, he will probably recite one in which he took a star part or where there was an unusual result or dramatic finish. In my case, I feel my fondest memory is of the events at Rottingdean in October, 1966.

The story centres around Rottingdean Cricket Club and a remarkable character Tony Salisbury, who was captain and leading light of the Club which, established in 1758, is one of the oldest in the country. Rottingdean is a small village, a few miles to the east of Brighton, sandwiched between hills with the sea to the south and farmland to the north. The ground is on the north side, a few hundred yards up a well-worn path from 'The Plough', next to the village pond.

There is a fabulous legend about an incident in a match at Rottingdean a hundred or more years ago, when the pitch used to be at the top of a hill, near the existing windmill. The players could look out to sea and a batsman, obviously a super-star, held up play for twenty minutes, because a sailing ship was passing behind the bowler's arm! Clearly the concept of *stars* and *domestics* was as valid then as it is now.

Nowadays they have a smart modern pavilion, but in the early sixties they only had an old wooden shack. Basically a larger scale model of the Eskdale one I detailed in an earlier chapter, it had splintered floor and primitive ablutions, all to classic rustic specification. Due to a lack of windows, the visiting side had to stumble about in near darkness when changing but also in one corner stood a huge Victorian wardrobe. This massive mahogany and glass creation was a frightening booby-trap to the unsuspecting visitor. In the usual absence of pegs, a player would innocently open the mirrored doors with alarming results, as the whole thing would tip slowly forwards crushing him beneath a hundred-weight of wood and glass.

Tony Salisbury was a tall slim Old Etonian, always bubbling over with enthusiasm for the game and a real asset to any club. He was undoubtedly the most generous cricketer in the bar that I have ever known, although he rarely if ever, bought anyone a pint. He simply bought a jug. He was an avid gambler, ready to wager a quid on the most unlikely prospect and the escapades he got involved in were many and legendary.

To recall one, he was on a tour to the Isle of Wight when he went out for a stroll along the promenade with a few colleagues to look over the talent on the beach before the match. Being the height of the holiday season, there were hundreds of people sunbathing and as they were wandering along, Salisbury spotted a scaffold-type jetty going out to sea about thirty yards and used by the pleasure boats for mooring purposes. Immaculately dressed as always, Salisbury guaranteed that for a quid a head, he would dive in from the jetty fully clothed. Bets were soon sealed and pausing only to remove his jacket and tie, he rushed down the beach, along the jetty and dived in head first. Thinking it was some publicity stunt, the whole beach rose to their feet and applauded enthusiastically then clamoured round for his auto-graph as he reached the shore and ran back to his colleagues to collect his winnings. Without batting an eyelid, he pushed the pound notes into his soggy wallet and they continued their stroll as if nothing had happened. By the time they got to the ground Salisbury had more or less dried out, in one sense at least.

Although he scored a lot of runs in club cricket, Tony Salisbury was not, in my opinion, a star in the true sense. I would really classify him as an alternating star or domestic for the following reasons. When he went into bat, he was always extremely nervous and for the first ten minutes or so, would grope, edge and lunge shakily, while trying to play himself in according to the text book. This was all rather painful to watch, but suddenly he would get fed-up with all the theory and lift a perfectly good length ball straight over the sight-screen. From then on everything happened at once, as he either amassed a huge score or holed out to the furthest corner of the ground.

In order to get the record straight about the end of the 1966 season, I thought I ought to get hold of the Rottingdean score book for that year. Being such a venerable club, I expected to have to make an appointment to visit the archives and be ushered to a seat among rows of dusty score books by an elderly uniformed attendant. Thankfully, in true club cricket tradition it was not quite like that. I am indebted to many members of the club, who joined me in a sleuth-like search in the attics of Rottingdean, which would have tested the combined talents of James Bond and Charlie Barlow. Good fun as it was, we never did find the score book, so I had to resort to phone calls, pub crawls and much chin-fingering and head-scratching. Anyway, all that matters now is the gist of the story, which I think is roughly correct.

I turned up for the last listed fixture of the season at Rottingdean on Sunday, October 2nd, playing for the opposition NALGO. It was a reasonable day with a fair proportion of blue sky, although the summer as a whole had been a poor one. Tony Salisbury had had his best season with the bat, reckoning that he had scored 927 runs, and jokingly invited us to toss up some friendly ones so that he could reach his thousand for the first time in his career. He knew of course that he was unlikely to make 73 but did quite well and scored 32 before he holed out to long-on.

The old pavilion did not incorporate a bar, so we trooped off down to the 'Plough' around seven o'clock to celebrate the end of the season. It had a marvellous intimate atmosphere, with full-height oak panelling, lots of cosy alcoves and a minimum of window area, and with dimmed lighting and small floor space

Deedee

Tony Salisbury in action on the Isle of Wight
'pausing only to remove . . .' 'clamoured round for autographs . . .'

everyone was crammed together in a conspiratorial huddle. Apart from a certain melancholy because of the end of the season, it soon became clear that Salisbury was genuinely disappointed at not reaching his thousand runs. The great Peter Beecheno was playing for Rottingdean on this occasion and in an inspired move, suddenly strode over to the door and peered out for a few seconds into the near darkness. He returned and stated with convincing authority that the 'clouds were high' and on that sound meteorological basis, next Sunday was certain to be a fine day. Why not, therefore, play another match?

Within minutes, Beecheno's XI was formed, all arrangements made and the atmosphere and beer consumption rate improved dramatically. True enough, Sunday, October 9th, was a bright, fine day, with the pitch firm and the match got under way at 1.30. It was an enjoyable and hard fought game, but when Salisbury got to the wicket, disaster of disasters, he lunged forward and was caught behind for nought.

Again we trooped off down to the 'Plough' and with a 6.30 finish, we had to wait till opening time at seven o'clock. The evening was almost a carbon copy of the previous week, Beech

'The clouds are high!'

once again making his prophetic weather forecast and his XI
was formed for Sunday, October 16th, one o'clock start.

Once again Beech was right and we got started on another
cold but fine day with the track firmed up by a touch of frost on
top. This time Salisbury could muster only 23 runs, before he got
out still leaving him eighteen short of the target.

With a six o'clock finish, we had to hang around to opening
time, but nevertheless, another fine session developed in the
'Plough' and this time Mike Bowring from Cuckfield volunteered
to form Bowring's XI for Sunday, October 23rd, 12.30 start.
Some far-sighted soul pointed out that Salisbury would have to
score the runs on the 23rd, because apart from anything else, the
clocks went back on the 30th and it would be dark by 4.30.

Being an indolent youth at the time, I used to lie-in on Sunday
mornings and got up around 10.30 for breakfast on the morning

of the 23rd. Immediately afterwards, I got ready to go out for the match and I still recall the few seconds before I left home. I was living with my parents at the time and they used to enjoy the comfort of a coal fire on a winter Sunday. As I passed the living room door, I called out that I was off for the day, and probably wouldn't be back till late. My father bent double doing some nifty poker-work on the fire, asked as an after-thought where I was going. When I replied, he stood up abruptly, peered out of the window, then at the cricket bag I was holding and finally studied a calendar on the wall. He raised his eyebrows, shrugged his shoulders and without saying a word, powerfully transmitted the comment, 'Well, if you want to be a bloody fool, I suppose I can't stop you.'

When I got to Rottingdean, the pitch, aided by a hard frost, turned out to be as fast as it had been all season in the opinion of the home side. The match developed into a real cliff-hanger, as Bowring's XI batted first and were all out for 95. Salisbury put himself in at number three in the batting order and tension mounted rapidly when the openers raced away and put on over 50 for the first wicket. Fortunately he got to the crease around 4.30, although by then he looked decidedly the worse for wear after a heavy Saturday night session, followed by a few more jars during the lunch interval. With the bowler under strict instructions to produce the friendliest half-volleys and avoid the stumps at all costs, Salisbury swished and lunged painfully, accumulating runs slowly off snicks and mis-hits. When he had scored 12, he launched out and skied a catch to cover, and every-one was dumbstruck when they realized that the fielder, a last minute fill-in, had probably not been fully briefed on the situation. He certainly made a determined effort to hold the catch, but happily ended up rolling on the ground, parted from the ball by a few feet. To cheers and audible sighs of relief, Salisbury scored 18 and reached his thousand just before Rottingdean knocked off the runs to win the match.

With the game over by 5.30 a prospective hour-and-a-half wait for opening time was not really on, and some people went home, promising to return later. A dozen of us wandered down to the 'Plough' around six o'clock, whereupon some inconsiderate lout hammered on the door and awakened the frightened landlord from his Sunday afternoon nap. Salisbury, exercising his limitless charm, suggested that one or two players could be booked in as residents and also drew his attention to the unusually thick curtains in the bar upstairs. Eventually ushered in, we started the most euphoric evening in my cricket career. Closeted in the dimly lit upper bar, I know for a fact that we got through nine jugs, or seventy-two pints of bitter in the hour before opening time, plus goodness knows how much thereafter. The euphoria was enhanced in my case as I won the jackpot on the fruit machine, thereby financing my contribution to the kitty.

Going home along the seafront around eleven o'clock I recall a feeling of complete contentment. We had cheated the winter by stretching the cricket season nearly into November, had had a fine game, and Salisbury had reached his target. On top of that we had finished with an uninhibited session in a pub deep in the heart of an historic old English village. In retrospect, it was perhaps a latter-day re-enactment of part of 'England Their England'.

I must add that there is an unhappy postscript to this tale. One of the Rottingdean players was checking the club averages a week or two later and found out that Salisbury had miscounted his original run total, and had not actually reached his thousand runs. Fortunately, Beech was not at the meeting, otherwise no doubt he would have ambled across to the door and peered up at the sky: 'The clouds are high'.

Turning to the future I'm constantly reminding myself that Jack Hobbs scored more centuries after his 40th birthday than before it. I suppose he had a slight edge talent-wise but I'm hopeful that by that time I may be able to bridge the gap by sheer weight of experience. Ideally I would like to end up in a position similar to the hero of a charming tale related to me by a player from Hailsham last year. The Hailsham 2nd XI arranged a fixture against a tiny mid-Sussex village that no-one had ever heard of before. It was one of those places reached by a dead-end cart track, with the signposts, if any, legible only with the aid of a magnifying glass. When the Hailsham side eventually located the pitch the hero of the story, whom I shall call Old Joe, was busy with the roller and whitewash on his own in the middle of the ground.

The Hailsham team got changed and when their skipper went out to find his opposite number, Old Joe came forward. With Hailsham batting first, Old Joe immediately put himself on at the bottom end, from where he tossed up his friendly off-breaks

By Courtesy: J. Winchcombe

Nostalgia: the changing room in the old Rottingdean pavilion. This vintage flash photo shows the dark pegless room with mahogany wardrobe awaiting its next victim.

unchanged through to the interval. Queuing up in the pavilion for the usual sandwich and cakes, once again Old Joe was in action, this time behind the counter pouring out cups of tea.

By now highly intrigued, the Hailsham players watched the pavilion door intently when they took the field and sure enough out came Old Joe to open the batting. He had no strokes but occupied the crease in a world of his own for a long time before he was eventually removed. When they got changed after the match, Old Joe was the obvious person to ask for guidance to the local and he readily obliged, pointing out the 'Spotted Dog' some fifty yards down the road. Having assembled themselves and made the short journey, they entered this quaint old pub, and who should they find busily pulling pints behind the bar? Good Old Joe.

Now the proud father of a son and daughter I am reasonably confident that in a dozen years or so, my boy will be groping forward and swishing around like his old man. We recently celebrated his fourth birthday, and before the day I found out that his main present was to be a large size automatic machine-gun. Deciding that the world had gone mad, I exercised my prerogative as head of the household and cancelled the order with instructions that his present should be a miniature cricket set.

On his birthday I took a look out of the window and decided to get in some practice immediately. I explained to Mark that the sticks were called stumps and that the bat was held at the thin black end. With my daughter Lisa, aged six, we went out into the back garden, where I selected the roughest patch of grass I could find and set up the stumps. I then stood Mark in front with masses of instructions as to what to do and bribed Lisa to stand at a wide-ish mid-on with the offer of a lollipop.

I paced out a full length run-up and then in my quicker style, raced in for my first delivery. It was a pearler, swinging late in the air, whipping back across, pitching and lifting viciously. Mark took a belated swing and was bowled all over the place.

Another *domestic* in the making! ! !

J. Hindmarsh

The author passing on the fundamentals of the game to his children

The Domestic Glossary

adv	adverb
abb	abbreviation
a.d	alternative definition
ch	chapter

col	colloquialism
n	noun
v	verb

Bails (! !)
An expletive; for use in mixed company

Bazooka attack (col)
A series of high altitude deliveries, to test the batsman's long range vision

Beamer (n)
A swift full-bunger, aimed to decapitate

Bent (adv)
To lean heavily towards one side

Blob (n)
A duck

Blonger (n)
A blob, a duck *(see: blob)*

Bouncer (n)
A fast short pitched ball occasionally delivered by a berserk domestic bowler (*a.d* An affable and kindly dance hall attendant)

Boundary (n)
That point in the outfield beyond which one cannot proceed without cutting tools or mechanical equipment

Boundary marker (n)
A piece of old rag, nailed to a stick, previously licked with white emulsion

Box (n)
A receptacle for personal effects

Buzz (n)
A fast flat return to the stumps (*a.d* a telephone call)

Caress (v)
To slide the leather erotically across the greensward

Castle (v)
To knock over the woodwork, i.e. bowl comprehensively

Chinaman (v)
A velly clever ball

Coerce (v)
To chastise, whip or smack with the willow

Cow (n)
An ugly agricultural shot, with no aesthetic merit

Cream (v)
To plunder any loose or indifferent bowling

Crease (v)
To double up in hysterical mirth

Daisy Cutter (n)
A shooter or grubber, a fatal ball to a swinging domestic

Domestic (n)
An esoteric term for a player who does not expect to influence the course of events in a match *(see: Ch. 2)*

Donkey Drop (n)	A domestic bowler's cunningly disguised slower ball
Drop Anchor (v)	Modern jargon for stonewalling or blocking
Duck (n)	A blob, a blonger *(see: blob)*
Family Affair (n)	Father umpire, son fast bowler
Fend (v)	Exercise of the martial arts with the bat
Finger Happy (adv)	An umpire prone to frequent and instantaneous dismissals
Full-bunger (n)	A high full toss (potentially lethal to domestic batsmen)
'Ger on wiv it!' (col)	An erudite impassioned plea to the batsman to elevate the scoring rate
'Gi'e it tap, lud!' (col)	(Northern origin). Freely translated as an exhortation to the batsmen to commence a virulent assault on the bowling
'Give it some stick!' (col)	To cane the bowling with unabashed brutality
'Give it the charge!' (col)	To thunder down the track in a frontal assault
'Give it the ol' heave-ho!' (col)	A joyous entertaining mixture of heaves and ya-hoo's
'Go deep!' (v)	A vague instruction to a fielder, to ruminate in the rough
Google (v)	Verbalisation of the googly (for definition: see more learned works)
Grass (v)	To drop a catch *(a.d* an informant, a soft drug)
Grope (n)	Basic defensive shot of domestic batsman—played well forward, off balance, with head up and bat away from pad *(a.d* a furtive manual exploration)
Hammer (v)	To strike the ball with explosive and primeval force
'Hari-kari job!' (n)	The frenetic and suicidal pursuit of quick runs—for the good of the side
Heave (n)	A mechanically inefficient shot, i.e. high energy input for little discernible result
Hoik (v)	To ladle the ball in ungainly fashion
Hole-out (v)	To be caught short
Hook (n)	A rusty nail occasionally found on the dressing room wall

In-ducker (n)	A ball which swings in late to the batsman (not negotiable by a domestic)
Jock (n)	A type of guardhouse, i.e. a structure to restrain the privates (a.d someone who lives north of Watford)
Jug-shot (n)	An involuntary run scoring stroke by a batsman on 49
Kitty (n)	A collectivised purchasing system, whereby a third of a pint of lukewarm bitter is obtained for 20p
Knock (v)	A star plays an innings, but a domestic has a knock
L.b.w. (abb)	Luxurious breaking of wind
Lunge (n)	A type of desperation grope, played as, or after the ball passes the bat (a.d upper-crust pronunciation of dinner)
Maiden (n)	Rarely seen nowadays in club cricket
'Middle from where 'e bowls' (col)	A request by a batsman for a guard to be given from the bowler's usual delivery position
'Nought for plenty' (col)	Typical domestic bowling analysis
'One for the off' (col)	A contrived friendly first ball to a new batsman, to assist him to 'open the account'
Outfield (n)	That area of the ground where the grass can only be cut with a scythe
'Pad up' (v)	The process of girding the loins in preparation for combat (a.d the noble self-sacrifice of limbs to prevent leather hitting wood)
Pearler (n)	A deceptively quick ball which ducks in late, pitches, whips back across and lifts viciously (n.b. the usual terminal delivery to a star)
Ping (v)	To despatch the ball with flippant and contemptuous indifference
Prod (n)	A stabbing forward joust (a.d action sequential to a successful grope)
Pull (n)	Necessary movement of the forearm to replenish a glass
Punch (v)	A shot struck with piston-like movement of the right forearm (n.b. for left-handers, read left forearm)

'Push it about' *(col)*	An innings of indolent and facile economy
'Put down a dolly' *(col)*	To drop a simple catch *(a.d to cease man-handling an attractive young lady)*
Rabbit (n)	A virgin performer, undefiled by talent, technique or experience
Rogue buzz (n)	A wild mis-directed throw, wreaking havoc and carnage amongst the close field
Scorer (n)	A domestic's wife capable of putting two and two together
Shocker (n)	A star batsman's description of an l.b.w. decision
Shooter (n)	A domestic batsman's explanation of an l.b.w. decision
Shout (n)	A discreet invitation to the umpire to consider the adjacency
Sight-screen (n)	A piece of torn grey canvas designed to flap behind the bowler's arm and distract the batsman
Skipper's round (n)	An obsolescence, a thing of the past
Slash (v)	To despatch the ball with a vicious late karate chop (n.b. perfected by Jim E. Riddle, Lancs. and England)
Slog (n)	An innings with a high proportion of heaves, cows, tonks and ya-hoo's
Smear (n)	A ferocious cross-batted heave to leg
Smear (v)	To play an innings of violent, but effective, inelegance
Snick (n) or (v)	The fortuitous result of a grope
Snorter (n)	A vicious, venemous delivery, unplayable by any batsman
Squirt (n)	A belated shot squeezing the ball away from the stumps *(a.d the young son of a gentleman)*
Star (n)	A player possessed of talent and confidence, who expects to influence the course of events *(see: Ch 2)*
Steer (v)	To deflect the ball with geometric precision *(a.d something to do with the bum)*
Swing (n)	An unfettered smooth circular motion of the bat *(a.d unwitting and uncontrollable aerial movements by a domestic bowler)*

Swoop (n)	A one-handed hawkish lunge at the ball by a fielder, demonstrating athleticism, aggression and other noble qualities (n.b. an impressive ploy by a domestic providing care is taken to avoid contact with the ball)
'Take apart' (v)	To disembowel the bowling attack with clinical precision
'There or thereabouts' (col)	A succession of accurate deliveries virtually eliminating scoring strokes
Thrash (v)	To humiliate and desecrate the bowling (*a.d* one hell of a binge)
Ton (n)	A star's practical intent, a domestic's illusive dream
Tonk (n)	A lusty full-bodied blow
Waft (n)	A nebulous air-shot, avoiding contact by wide margins of time and space
'Well left' (col)	A derogoratory compliment to a batsman after a non-connecting grope (*see* Beech, ch. 3)
Ya-hoo (n)	A naïve exhuberant swing, refreshingly free from technical inhibitions
Yorker (n)	A ball which pitches under a ya-hoo
'Yours' (col)	The correct call by a domestic fielder in the vicinity of a difficult high catch